A COMPANION TO

THE NEW SCOFIELD REFERENCE BIBLE

A Companion to
THE NEW SCOFIELD
REFERENCE
BIBLE

E. SCHUYLER ENGLISH

New York   OXFORD UNIVERSITY PRESS   1972

TO
R. H. E.
A Gift from God

Preface

Many people would like to know the Bible better but do not know how to go about it. Even those who own a Bible with helps, like The New Scofield Reference Bible, sometimes find it difficult to fit all the parts of Scripture into their proper place. Often this is due to their lack of training or because for some years they have not disciplined themselves to study. This book is written especially for these people.

The author's purpose is to present in one compact volume an over-all view of God's revelation to men as it is made known in the Scriptures. The reader is taken from the beginnings of the world and the creation of man to the consummation of all things in Christ, who is shown to be the central theme of the Bible and of all history. This book, which is a companion to The New Scofield Reference Bible and should be used in conjunction with it, will help the reader bring into focus the perfect harmony of the Scriptures and thus gain an understanding of the Bible as a whole.

Valuable assistance in preparing the *Companion* was given me by all the surviving members of the editorial committee of The New Scofield Reference Bible, namely, Doctors William Culbertson, Charles L. Feinberg, Frank E. Gaebelein, Allan A. MacRae, Clarence E. Mason, Jr., Wilbur M. Smith, and John F. Walvoord. Each of these distinguished scholars took time to read virtually every word of the original manuscript. Their thoughtful criticisms and suggestions helped a great deal. To work with these men again was a source of pleasure and an intellectual stimulus.

In fairness to them, however, I must stress that the final responsibility for the contents of the book is mine alone.

Appreciation is due the publishers for their encouragement and co-operation. I am also indebted to my long-time friend and secretary, Mrs. Joan B. Smith, who typed the manuscript and faithfully checked every Scripture reference for me.

Skytop, Pa.   E. SCHUYLER ENGLISH
May 27, 1971

Contents

A COMPANION TO

THE NEW SCOFIELD REFERENCE BIBLE

Introduction:
Using The New Scofield Reference Bible

A REFERENCE Bible has been described as "a tool for understanding the most important of all books." A tool is ineffective if it lies idle. Even the most sophisticated implements of our technological age must be used to be effectual. So with The New Scofield Reference Bible.

God, who has spoken to man in His Son, the incarnate Word, also speaks in the Bible, His written Word. It is the Christ of the Bible in whom God's Person is made known. It is the Scriptures that reveal His divine attributes and program. Without any man-made helps but by reading and studying the Bible under the guidance of the Holy Spirit myriads of men and women have learned about God's ways and will. However, aids that are the outcome of years of study facilitate the understanding of the Bible. Such helps must never in any way be confused with the Scriptures themselves. With this in mind, use the helps presented in The New Scofield Reference Bible (hereinafter designated NSRB) as a guide in your Bible study. The following synopsis will serve as a manual.

I. *The Text*

The translation used in the NSRB is the King James Version with, as the title page shows, "such word changes . . . as will help the reader." These changes pertain generally to English words or phrases that are archaic, have become obsolete, or have altered their meaning during the more than 350 years since the

King James Version (hereinafter designated KJV) was translated from the original languages.

Virtually all the major changes in the Bible text are indicated by thin perpendicular lines shown on either side of the new expression, and the KJV word or phrase stands in the margin. For illustration, see page 57, Gen. 40:17 ^{p}|foods|, where the margin at p reads KJV *bakemeats*; p. 248, Dt.28:27 ^{l}|boil|, margin at l, KJV *botch*; p.998, Mt.5:15 ^{n}|lampstand|, margin at n, KJV *candlestick*; p.1221, Rom.8:16 ^{j}|himself|, margin at j, KJV *itself*; p.1299, 1Tim. 4:12 ^{cc}|conduct|, margin at cc, KJV *conversation*.

Some personal pronouns have been changed, e.g. "his" to "its" when the usage refers to inanimate objects. In Exodus 37:20 the KJV's "his knops, and his flowers" reads "its ^{e}|knobs|, and its flowers" in the NSRB. The relative pronoun "which" is altered to "who" or "whom" when it alludes to persons, e.g. Mt. 6:9. There are other minor substitutions like "here" and "there" for "hence" and "thence" respectively. Generally no notice of substitutions of this nature is placed in the margin.

Obsolete spelling has been brought up to date in the NSRB, e.g. "musick" to "music," "throughly" to "thoroughly," "shew" to "show," "plaister" to "plaster." Here again notice is not given in the margin.

Proper nouns have been up-dated according to the best texts, like "Phenicia" to "Phoenicia," and in the New Testament the Greek forms of the Old Testament Hebrew names have been brought into conformity with their use in the O.T., e.g. "Elias" to "Elijah," "Eliseus" to "Elisha," "Esaias" to "Isaiah." A list of changes of this kind is presented in the back of the NSRB, pp. 1388–92.

In common with some other editions of the English Bible the use of italics in the text of the NSRB indicates that the words italicized are not present in the original languages but have been supplied by translators to clarify the meaning.

A simplified system of self-pronunciation has been introduced to facilitate public reading. The key to pronunciation symbols may be found on p. xiv.

4

2. *Subheadings*

Subheadings appear along with the Bible text on every page. Because these headings have been supplied by the editors they are printed in italics and in a type size smaller than the text, so that they will not be confused with Scripture.

The purpose of the headings is

(a) to carry through each book of the Bible the outline given in the introduction to that book, for example pp. 941–43, headings above Jonah 1:1,12; 3:1; 4:1;

(b) to guide the reader concerning the sense of the passage immediately following the heading, e.g. p. 934, above Amos 4:1,6;

(c) to indicate parallel passages of Scripture, e.g. p. 1019, above Matthew 15:10, which refers to Mark 7:14–23;

(d) to help locate quickly certain portions of the Bible, e.g. p. 1179; and

(e) to draw attention to other vital Scriptures that illuminate the immediate text, e.g. heading above Galatians 5:17, which points the reader to Romans 8:2 and an explanatory footnote at Romans 7:15.

3. *Margins*

The marginal notations give help in a number of ways:

(a) There are cross references to other Scriptures which relate to the subject at hand, e.g. Rom. 6:8, margin *h*.

(b) A literal translation of a word or phrase may be shown, e.g. Rom. 6:10, margin *j*.

(c) Alternative renditions of the text or explanatory comments may be given, as at Romans 6:6, margin *e* and Romans 6:19, margin *o*.

(d) Chain references are denoted, e.g. Rom. 6:8, margin *g*; 6:9, margin *i*; see also *q, u, v, w*. More information about the chain references appears in section 4 below.

(e) KJV readings are given, as has been explained above, e.g. Rom. 7:8, margins *r* and *s*.

5

(f) Dates are supplied, when they are known, at the top of the column in the O.T. and the top of the left-hand column in the N.T. as well as at the chapter and verse on the same page to which a date specifically applies. For examples see p. 412, top of column, and at margin *f* related to verse 9 and *gg* related to verse 25; p. 1160, top of left column, and at margin *e* related to verse 3.

4. *Chain References*

The chain references in the margin offer an important key to an understanding of the Bible. Seventy-three subjects are traced from the first allusion to each subject to the last, with a summary footnote either at the last reference or at an appropriate text somewhere within the chain.

As an illustration, see p. 365, margin *p* from 2 Samuel 7:16:

> *p Kingdom*
> (O.T.): vv.
> 8–16; 2 Sam.
> 23:1. (Gen.
> 1:26; Zech.
> 12:8)

The subject is the Kingdom in the O.T.; the notation vv. 8–16 refers to the location of the subject matter on this page; 2 Sam. 23:1 tells where the next reference to Kingdom (O.T.) may be found. The first reference within the parentheses, Gen. 1:26, denotes where the chain begins; the second, Zech. 12:8, where the chain closes and the summary note appears. The reader can start at Genesis 1:26 (where see margin *a*), from there go on to Genesis 9:6, from there to Exodus 3:1, and so on to the final references to Kingdom (O.T.) at Zechariah 12:8 where, at ¹David, he is directed to a footnote on the same page, which carries a summary of what the Bible teaches on the subject.

In some instances, because the summary note does not appear at the last Bible reference to the subject, the second marginal reference within the parentheses includes the word *note*. For example see p. 1124, margin *h* from John 1:14:

> *h Grace*
> vv. 14,
> 16,17;
> Acts 4:
> 33. (Jn. 1:
> 14; Jn. 1:
> 17, *note*)

Here the subject is Grace; the notation vv. 14, 16, 17 alludes to the location of the subject matter on this page; Acts 4:33 tells where the next reference to Grace may be found. The first reference within the parentheses shows where the chain begins (in this case right here in verse 14). The second reference within the parentheses does not designate the last mention of the subject but takes the reader to the summary footnote which is at the foot of this same page, from ^{1h}grace at John 1:17. However, the chain references carry on to the last mention of grace, Revelation 22:21.

A complete list of subjects covered in the chain references is shown on pp. 1378–79. This tabulation may be used as a basis for serious study of some of the major Bible themes. See also p. xiv.

5. *Annotations*

There are three areas of annotations in the NSRB: (a) introductions to the various divisions of the Bible, (b) an introduction to each book of the Bible, and (c) footnotes throughout the Bible.

(a) The Bible is one book. Yet it is composed of sixty-six separate books, thirty-nine in the O.T. and twenty-seven in the N.T. The O.T. and the N.T. are also divided into other sections. The O.T. has four major divisions: the Pentateuch—the first five books of the Bible, which are also known as the Law or the Books of Moses; the Historical Books—Joshua to Esther; the Books of Poetry and Wisdom—Job to Song of Solomon (Lamentations is generally assigned to this section also); and the Prophetic

Books—Isaiah to Malachi (except Lamentations). The N.T. falls into four divisions also: the four Gospels, The Acts, the Epistles, and The Revelation.

The NSRB carries introductions to most of the major divisions of the Bible, e.g. The Pentateuch, p. xvi; The Historical Books, p. 258; The Four Gospels, pp. 987–89. In addition, a history of the Jewish nation during the approximately four centuries between the writing of the last book of the O.T. (Malachi) and the first book of the N.T. (Matthew) is given on pp. 983–84.

The introductions to the various divisions of the Bible should be kept in mind in the study of any section of Scripture. Here A Panoramic View of the Bible, pp. ix–xi, will provide an essential overview of Scripture as a whole.

(b) Before any individual book of the Bible is studied, the introductory remarks should be read thoroughly. They show the name of the author (when it is known), the theme of the book, and the date of writing (when this information is available). The introduction also summarizes the book, points out its key verses or passages in many instances, and gives an outline. See, for illustration, pp. 1 and 991.

(c) Most pages of the NSRB carry footnotes. Their diversity is wide. Doctrines are defined and summarized. There are notes on the divine covenants, e.g. Gen. 12:2; dispensations, e.g. Gen. 1:28 (at heading); historical notes, e.g. Isa. 36:1; and archaeological notes, e.g. 2 Ki. 7:6. Words are defined in their biblical use. See footnotes at Mt. 22:16; 24:34; Eph. 1:11; 1 Pet. 1:20. biblical measures and weights are shown, 2 Chr. 2:10; Acts 27:28, as is the approximate value of coinage in biblical times, Ex. 30:13; Mt. 5:26. The typical meanings of O.T. persons and inanimate objects are explained, e.g. Ex. 28:1; Lev. 1:9. Matters relating to biblical criticism are discussed, for instance the Mosaic authorship of Deuteronomy, Dt. 31:24; 2 Ki. 22:8. Meanings of parables, Mt. 13:44; music in the Bible, 1 Chr. 15:16; the chronological order of the prophets, p. 712; the doctrine of tongues, 1 Cor. 14:27; and prophecies in the Bible, e.g. Isa. 41:2; Dan. 8:17; 9:24; 12:4, are among the variety of footnotes spaced throughout the

8

NSRB, each one appearing in the place where it is most needed. There are more than eighty notes concerning the Person, attributes, and activities of the Lord Jesus Christ. For handy reference about a particular subject, consult the Index to Annotations at the back of the volume, pp. 1380–87.

6. *Concordance*

Also at the back of the NSRB, numbered pp. 1–188, is a Concise Concordance to proper nouns, subject matter, and key words of the Bible, which has been specially prepared to take into account the word changes in the text. To discover the location of a Scripture text, refer to a familiar word or phrase in that passage. As an illustration, if the location of the expression "the law was our schoolmaster to bring us to Christ" is desired, it may be found by consulting the concordance for key words like "law" or "schoolmaster," under which it is shown that the reference is Galatians 3:24.

7. *Maps*

New Oxford Bible maps are included at the very end of the NSRB. These maps are particularly useful in connection with the study of historical passages of Scripture. The index to them appears on pp. 189–92 of the concordance.

The Ultimate Authority

Finally, let it be emphasized that the Bible text alone is the Word of God. Read it prayerfully, depending upon the Holy Spirit as the guide into the truth (Jn. 16:13). To gain the maximum value from the marginal references and other annotations in the NSRB, it is essential that all Scripture references be looked up. The annotations are tools to help you understand the Bible. Utilize them fully and thoughtfully and you will grow in your knowledge of "the most important of all books."

CHAPTER I

About the Bible

THERE are many people, even among those who read the Bible faithfully, who are uninformed concerning its origin and history. Who wrote the Bible? How was it written? What were its original languages? How was it translated and by whom? Was it limited to the sixty-six books that now compose it and, if so, why? Where did the English Bible come from?

1. *Who Wrote the Bible*

Some forty different men wrote the Bible over a period spanning approximately 1500 years, from about 1450 B.C. to about A.D. 90. These writers represent various levels of society and diverse backgrounds including kings, statesmen, prophets, priests, apostles, shepherds, a tax collector, a tentmaker, and a physician. God the Holy Spirit inspired their writing, for they did not speak only for themselves but "as they were moved by the Holy Spirit" (2 Pet. 1:21). This is why the Bible (derived from the Greek word *biblia*, meaning *books*) is called the Holy Bible. It is known by other names also, such as the Book, the Book of books, God's Word, the Holy Scriptures, and Scripture.

2. *Bible Manuscripts*

The original books of the Bible were not books as we know them today. They were manuscripts written by hand on parchment and papyrus. The earliest manuscripts were inscribed on stone and clay. Following these, parchment made from skins of goats and sheep became the medium of written language until about the fourth century B.C., when the Egyptians, Greeks, and Romans began to substitute papyrus for parchment. Papyrus was made from the pith or tissue of a plant of the same name. It was cross-woven like basket material and fashioned into sheets that could be rolled. Most of the New Testament was written on this material.

None of the original manuscripts of the Bible is known to exist today. This is hardly astonishing. There are no known original manuscripts of any of the classical writers of antiquity, such as Plato, Cicero, and Herodotus. Bible manuscripts, however, are generally dated much nearer to the original documents than those of other ancient writings. For whereas the interval of time between the writing of the ancient classics and the existing manuscripts averages about 1000 years, the elapsed time between the original documents of the N.T. and existing manuscripts is closer to 250 years. Furthermore, the number of extant ancient manuscripts of sacred writings is much greater than in the case of secular works.

Until a little more than twenty years ago the oldest known manuscript of the Old Testament was dated somewhere in the ninth century A.D., the whole O.T., A.D. 1010. Then came the discovery in 1947 of the Dead Sea Scrolls at Qumran in Palestine. Among the more than 500 manuscripts and fragments is a virtually complete scroll of Isaiah. Thus the age of the earliest known O.T. manuscript has been advanced about 1000 years, for the Dead Sea Scrolls date back to around 150 B.C.

The oldest extant N.T. writing consists of some papyrus fragments of the Gospel of John that are estimated to have been made during the first half of the second century A.D.

Since there was no such thing as a printing press in ancient times, copies of manuscripts were made by hand. Sometimes a scribe copied a single document several times. The work was done with supreme care to avoid error. Words and even letters were counted. Even so, mistakes crept in sometimes for several reasons: the writing being copied might not be legible to the scribe copying it, fatigue might have interfered with the accuracy of the scribe, or other factors to which humans are prone might have entered.

Not always was the oldest available manuscript necessarily the best one. It might have been copied by an inferior scribe. Or a document dated later might be only a third copy, whereas its earlier counterpart might be a fifth copy and therefore subject to more copyists' slips. For this reason manuscripts were chosen with extreme care. Selectivity of this kind holds today in regard to texts used in the translation of the Scriptures, the texts being evaluated by competent textual scholars.

3. *Bible Languages*

Virtually all of the O.T. was written in Hebrew, the language of the Jewish people. Small portions were set down in Aramaic (Chaldean), the language of ancient Syria. Both languages use the same alphabet. They are quite similar to one another in other respects also. Ezra 4:8–6:18; 7:12–26 were written in Aramaic, as were Jeremiah 10:11 and Daniel 2:4–7:28. A few Aramaic words appear even now in the English N.T., for example *Talitha cumi* (Mk. 5:41), *Ephphatha* (Mk. 7:34), *Cephas* (Jn. 1:42), and *Maran-atha* (1 Cor. 16:22).

Hebrew writing runs from right to left rather than from left to right. Here is a Hebrew sentence:

בְּרֵאשִׁית בָּרָא אֱלֹהִים אֵת הַשָּׁמַיִם וְאֵת הָאָרֶץ׃

which, transliterated into English characters, reads like this:

bᵉrēšîth bārā' 'ᵉlōhîm' ēth haśśāmayim wᵉ'eth hā'āreṣ

meaning

In the beginning God created the heavens and the earth.

In N.T. times the spoken tongue in Palestine was generally Aramaic and the written language Greek—not Attic or Classical Greek but *Koinē* Greek, the common language of the Greek-speaking world in the first century A.D. *Koinē* was based upon

Attic Greek but included many new words and forms of inflection. Whereas it is almost certain that our Lord and His disciples conversed in Aramaic, the N.T. was written in the *Koinē*. Here is a sentence in Greek:

Ἐν ἀρχῇ ἦν ὁ Λόγος, καὶ ὁ Λόγος ἦν πρὸς τὸν Θεόν, καὶ Θεὸς ἦν ὁ Λόγος.

which, transliterated, reads like this:

En arché ēn ho Lógos, kai ho Lógos ēn pros ton Theón, kai Theós ēn ho Lógos

meaning

In the beginning was the Word, and the Word was with God, and the Word was God.

4. *Early Bible Translations*

Because the Jewish people were scattered in various lands where Greek was the common written language, it became evident to godly Jews even before the time of Christ that their Bible (the O.T.) should be made available in Greek. It is almost certain that a vast number among the young people, who had never been in Israel, could neither read nor speak Hebrew. To translate the Scriptures into Greek was a work for men of dedicated scholarship. As a point of illustration, some Hebrew letters are quite similar to others. Observe how easy it might be to mistake

ר (r) for ד (d) or ו (v)

ב (b) for כ (k) or נ (n)

ה (h) for ח (kh) or ת (t)

To compound the problem, not only was early Hebrew written without vowels but also there was no space between words or sentences. Here is an English sentence that is familiar to millions, written in such a manner:

ndldsntnttmpttnbtdlvrsfrmvl

Bear in mind that in an early Hebrew manuscript such a line would not be set in type as it is here but written by hand, and even though it was put down with utmost care, there might be small variations in the formation of some letters. Here is the full sentence:

And lead us not into temptation, but deliver us from evil.

In the third century B.C. a company of devout and learned Jews began to translate the Hebrew O.T. into Greek. The work was not completed until around 180 B.C. Their translation is known as the Septuagint (from the Latin *septuaginta*, meaning *seventy*) because tradition suggests that seventy (or seventy-two) scholars undertook the work at the beginning. The Septuagint (abbreviated LXX, the Roman numeral for seventy) is still of unique value to Bible scholars. Many O.T. quotations in the N.T. are from the LXX.

Some say 72

About two centuries later Christ came to earth and the Church was born. The N.T. was written. Christianity spread throughout the Roman Empire. Because multitudes could read neither Hebrew nor Greek, a Latin Bible was needed. So, in the late fourth century A.D. a linguistic scholar, Jerome, began the translation of the whole Bible into Latin. Undertaking a task that was to consume nearly a quarter of a century, he began by revising existing Latin translations of some books in the Hebrew Canon. Although he worked primarily in Hebrew, he also consulted the LXX, as well as the N.T. in Greek and earlier Latin versions of the four Gospels. The task was completed about 404. Jerome's translation is called the Vulgate (from a Latin word meaning *common*, i.e. it is in colloquial language). For centuries the Vulgate has been used in services in the Roman Catholic Church, although recently the hierarchy authorized a revision of the Vulgate together with new translations of the Scriptures from original languages.

Other early translations from the Hebrew and Greek were the Syriac Version (Syriac is a branch of Aramaic), dated about the second century A.D., the Coptic (language of ancient Egypt and a form of Arabic), translated in portions from the third to the tenth centuries, and the Gothic (an early Teutonic language), begun sometime during the fourth century.

Christianity spread still further. In England, Latin was employed in church services even as late as the sixteenth century.

5. *The Bible in English*

Because the common people could neither read nor understand Latin, it came to pass that between the seventh and tenth centuries translations were made, mostly from the Vulgate, into the Anglo-Saxon tongue. Notable among these were the paraphrases of Caedmon and a translation by the Venerable Bede. Insofar as we know, no Old English Bible contained all sixty-six books of the O.T. and N.T. Then in the year 1382 John Wycliffe began his translation from the Vulgate into Middle English. This was a great step forward, but by the middle of the sixteenth century Middle English was difficult for the common people to understand. It was time for a new English Bible to make its appearance.

Meanwhile an event of surpassing importance had taken place. In Germany, a man named Johann Gutenberg had devised a way to use movable type in a printing press. The first full-length book from his press was a Latin edition of the Bible. It was printed in 1456. Until this time the Bible was still being written by hand. It required ten or more months to transcribe a single copy of the Bible. Now it could not only be printed in less time, but also hundreds or thousands of copies could be made at one printing. Gutenberg's invention marked a turning point, not only in the distribution of the Scriptures but also in the history of the world; for the printing press became the conveyer of literature and enlightenment to multitudes who, until then, had been dependent for their learning upon the reading of only a few privileged people.

Another important chapter in history was written when William Tyndale, after completing his studies at Oxford and Cambridge, decided to translate the Bible into English. The

Anglican Bishop of London refused to support him in this project, so Tyndale went to Germany and his N.T. translation was published there in 1525. Official opposition to his work was so great that copies of the N.T. had to be smuggled into England. He had also made some progress in work on the O.T., but he was betrayed, arrested, and put to death at Vilvorde, near Brussels, in 1536. While Tyndale was in prison Miles Coverdale took over his work and completed it in 1535. It is possible that Tyndale had the satisfaction of learning during his imprisonment that the complete Bible had been translated into readable English, so that, as he had expressed it years before, "the boy that drove the plough could know as much of the Scriptures as the Pope in Rome."

Other versions of the English Bible appeared rapidly: the Great Bible in 1539, the Geneva Bible in 1560, and the Bishop's Bible in 1568.

Until 1537 those who sat on the throne of England opposed free reading of the Scriptures. Then Henry VIII gave royal sanction to their wide dissemination. Other than for a few years during the reign of Mary I, when the English Bible was banned, it became increasingly appreciated and, in 1604, James I of England was requested by churchmen to authorize a new translation. This he did and in 1611 the King James Version (also known popularly as the Authorized Version) was published. This translation, done by forty-seven men of scholarship and spiritual acumen, has never been and perhaps never will be surpassed in the strength and beauty of its language. The King James Version is the greatest English classic. It is a masterpiece of first rank and has influenced the English language and literature for three and a half centuries as has no other book.

With the passing of the years the English language continued to change. To meet this need the Revised Version was published in Britain (the N.T. in 1881; the O.T. in 1885). Its basis was the King James Version, although of course the best manuscripts in the original languages of the Bible were consulted. Word changes were made to conform with the nineteenth-century English usage, and verb tenses were rendered with more accuracy than in the KJV. The text was divided into paragraphs rather than by verses, verse numbers being set within the paragraphs.* The Revised Version was followed in 1901 by the American Standard Version, which incorporates changes made by the American scholars who had shared in the work on the 1881–85 Revised Version.

Since the middle of the twentieth century there have been a number of new translations. There are reasons for this. The common man today has difficulty with some of the seventeenth-century English of the KJV. Earlier and more reliable manuscripts of the original languages of the Bible than were available in 1611 or even 1881 and 1901 have been found, textual scholarship has advanced, and archaeological discoveries of recent years have thrown much new light upon the Scriptures. Among the best-known Bibles that have been published within the last quarter of a century are the Revised Standard Version, a modern revision of the KJV (N.T. 1946; O.T. 1952), the Berkeley Version (N.T. 1945, revised 1969; O.T. 1959), the New English Bible (N.T. 1961; O.T. 1970), the Jerusalem Bible (English edition, 1966), the New American Bible (1970), and The New American Standard Bible, a modern revision of The American Standard Version of 1901 (N.T. 1960; O.T. 1971).† There have been quite a few translations and paraphrases of Scripture, done for the most part by individuals. Some of them have had a phenomenally wide distribution.

6. *The Canon*

Why is the Bible composed of just sixty-six books? Were there not other sacred writings? Who decided which books should be included in the Bible or excluded from it? The word "canon," which comes from a Greek noun meaning *a rule, a straight rod,* gives a clue.

*Chapter divisions did not appear in the Bible until A.D. 1250, when Cardinal Hugo marked them out as an aid to reference. In 1551 verse divisions began to be used so as to enable readers to locate specific passages of Scripture even more readily. The Geneva Bible (1560) was the first edition of the whole Bible to carry verse divisions.

†It is not the purpose of this book to point out the merits and demerits of these and other modern versions of the Scriptures, but simply to call attention to the lively interest in recent years in Bible translation and revision.

The last of the thirty-nine books of the O.T. was completed about 425 B.C. Present evidence suggests that the earliest N.T. writing may be dated around A.D. 45. Within that period of nearly 500 years other books were written that are known as the Apocrypha. This English word is taken over from the Greek *apokrýphon*, which means *hidden or secret*, and denotes a number of books that became a part of the LXX and Latin Bibles also.* The men who translated the KJV, following a precedent established by Miles Coverdale (1535) and Thomas Matthew (1537), included the Apocrypha as a separate section between the O.T. and the N.T. Today the Apocrypha is not generally included in copies of the Bible that are used by Protestants except in the Anglican or Episcopal Church, but it is officially part of the Bible used by Roman Catholics and some others.

The inclusion or exclusion of certain books as a portion of the written Word of God was not arbitrary but was established by standards of authenticity. The whole subject is complex and rather obscure. The process of determining the canonicity was probably a gradual one that extended over several generations in respect to both the O.T. and the N.T. What is known is that the O.T. canon was fairly well established by the fifth century B.C. and the N.T. finally sometime in the fourth century A.D. These canonical writings compose the sixty-six books of the Bible—thirty-nine in the O.T. and twenty-seven in the N.T. As for the Apocrypha, whereas these writings contain moral instruction, literary beauty, and historical information, the Protestant church as a whole does not construe them as being part of the divinely inspired Scriptures. Among the reasons for their rejection are the facts that the apocryphal books were not recognized by the Hebrews as a part of their Scriptures, and they are never cited in the N.T. Therefore, while they may be read with profit, they do not have divine authority and cannot be used to prove any point of Christian doctrine.

*The Apocrypha is composed of either fourteen or fifteen books, according to whether the Epistle of Jeremiah is incorporated with Baruch as its final chapter or as an individual book. The fifteen titles are: 1 Esdras, 2 Esdras, Tobit, Judith, Esther, The Wisdom of Solomon, Ecclesiasticus, Baruch, The Epistle of Jeremiah, The Song of Manasses, 1 Maccabees, 2 Maccabees.

• Different

Psuedopigraphal Books — false writing
DueteroCananical Books — 2nd Canon

7. *The Divisions of the Bible*

Although composed of many books, the Bible is a unity—one Book. Yet throughout the ages God has spoken in many portions and in many ways (cp. Heb. 1:1). There are two major divisions of the Bible—the O.T. and the N.T. And these two are themselves divided into different categories. For example Christ, in alluding to portions of the O.T., said, "Think not that I am come to destroy the law or the prophets" (Mt. 5:17). And again, "All things must be fulfilled which were written in the law of Moses, and in the prophets, and in the psalms, concerning me" (Lk. 24:44).

The divisions of the Bible may be summarized in this way:

A. The Old Testament

The O.T. is that portion of the Scriptures that God gave men before the birth of the Lord Jesus Christ. It records the creation of the world and of man, and traces man's history, including the choice of Israel as the nation that would be God's instrument of testimony to Himself on earth and the channel through which the Messiah should come, in whom all the nations of the earth would be blessed. Throughout the O.T. Christ may be seen in symbol and in prophecy. Concerning the O.T. writings He said, "Search the scriptures [meaning the O.T. since there was as yet no N.T. when He was on earth]; for in them ye think ye have eternal life; and they are they which testify of me" (Jn. 5:39).

The thirty-nine books of the English O.T. are divided into four segments,* as described in the pages which follow:

*The Hebrew Bible, comprising the O.T. only, is separated into three divisions—the Law, the Prophets, and the Writings—as follows: THE LAW: Genesis, Exodus, Leviticus, Numbers, Deuteronomy; THE PROPHETS: (*Former Prophets*) Joshua, Judges, 1 and 2 Samuel (as one book), 1 and 2 Kings (as one book); (*Latter Prophets*) Isaiah, Jeremiah, Ezekiel; and the twelve Minor Prophets (considered as one book)—Hosea, Joel, Amos, Obadiah, Jonah, Micah, Nahum, Habakkuk, Zephaniah, Haggai, Zechariah, Malachi; THE WRITINGS: Psalms, Proverbs, Job, Canticles, Ruth, Lamentations, Ecclesiastes, Esther, Daniel, Ezra and Nehemiah (as one book), 1 and 2 Chronicles (as one book).

a. The Pentateuch or Books of the Law

"Pentateuch," a combination of two Greek words, means *five books* and is a designation of the first five books of the Bible, Genesis to Deuteronomy. Our Lord Himself ascribed them to Moses. See NSRB, p. xvi; also *notes* at Ex. 17:14; Dt. 31;24; 2 Ki. 22:8. These books were known by the Hebrews as the Law (e.g. Mt. 7:12). Man's creation and fall into sin are shown in them. So also are God's redemption of man through grace, as prefigured in the sacrifices and offerings that pointed to the cross, and divine assurance concerning a coming Redeemer.

b. The Historical Books

The O.T. is a book rooted in history. Twelve of its thirty-nine books, namely Joshua to Esther, are aptly given the title Historical Books by scholars because they trace the history of the nation Israel for a period of about 1000 years, from 1450 to 425 B.C. See The Historical Books, NSRB, p. 258.

c. The Poetical and Wisdom Books

There are six of these—Job to Song of Solomon, plus Lamentations. Poetry does not mean that the text rhymes in sound or is written in metrical accent, as we know these devices. Rather, this designation has been given these books because they are written in Hebrew poetic forms and contain some of the most beautiful figures and imagery in world literature. Some of the greatest biblical poetry is in books not classed as poetical, for example Isaiah, Habakkuk, and Nahum.

Wisdom literature has to do first with the divine regulation evident in creation, which guides men and women as individuals, and whole nations. Second, it pertains to practical living on earth, whether in regard to family life, friendships, right versus wrong, etc., all being subject to the fear of the Lord. See The Poetical and Wisdom Books, NSRB, p. 571.

d. The Prophetic Books

There are sixteen books of prophecy in the O.T. beginning with Isaiah (omitting Lamentations, which is classified with the poetic writings) and running to Malachi at the end of the O.T. The prophetic books are often thought of as composing two sections: four major prophets—Isaiah to Daniel, and twelve minor prophets—Hosea to Malachi. The words "major" and "minor" do not allude to the importance of the messages of the prophets but to their length.

Prophecy is not only a foretelling of events but also a telling forth of the divine message. The Prophetic Books contain a great deal of both. By and large predictive prophecy has to do with the nation Israel. When Gentiles are mentioned it is usually in regard to their relationship with Israel. See The Prophetic Books, NSRB, pp. 711–12.

B. The New Testament

The N.T. is that portion of the Scriptures that God gave men after the birth, earthly life, crucifixion, resurrection, and ascension of the promised Messiah, our Lord Jesus Christ. It consists of twenty-seven books which record, in addition to Christ's ministry on earth, the descent of the Holy Spirit to the earth, the beginning and early history of the Church, instruction to the Church concerning this present age, and revelation of the consummation of all history and prophecy in the second coming of Christ and related events.

The twenty-seven books of the N.T. are divided into four categories:

a. The Four Gospels

The four Gospels—Matthew, Mark, Luke, and John—carry accounts of the first advent of Christ and His ministry, including His death and resurrection. These books are not four separate biographies of Jesus nor do the four of them together comprise His biography. Of our Lord's approximately thirty-three years on earth, His birth and surrounding events are given in some detail and there is an account of one incident in His twelfth year. Other than these, all that is written about Him in the Gospels pertains to His final three to three and a half years. About one-fourth of the Gospels pertains to Christ's final week on earth.

The first three Gospels are known as the Synoptic Gospels because they have much material in common and present a general synopsis of Christ's life and work. They give much space to His parables and miracles. The fourth Gospel contains important events not found in the Synoptics and includes major discourses not given in them. Over a third of John's Gospel pertains to the last week of Jesus' life.

Each of the four Gospels presents a different and significant aspect of Christ's Person: Matthew portrays Him as the promised King; Mark, as the Servant; Luke, as the Man; and John, as God the Son. Yet all four of them bear a united testimony to one unique Person—Jesus Christ, the Son of God and Redeemer of men. See The Four Gospels, NSRB, pp. 987–89.

b. The Acts

While in most copies of the Bible the title of the fifth book of the N.T. is written as The Acts of the Apostles, this book records the acts of the Holy Spirit through some of the apostles during the early years of the Church, beginning with Christ's ascension and the descent of the Holy Spirit on the day of Pentecost and terminating with the Apostle Paul's first imprisonment at Rome. It is, as it were, the bridge that carries the reader from the Gospels to the Epistles. See NSRB, p. 1160, the introduction to The Acts.

c. The Epistles

There are twenty-one epistles or letters in the N.T., beginning with Romans and concluding with Jude. The Epistles may be divided into three classifications: the thirteen Epistles of Paul, from Romans to Philemon; the Epistle to the Hebrews; and the seven General Epistles, James to Jude.

1. The Pauline Epistles develop a subject that was not known in O.T. times and was first mentioned by our Lord Jesus Christ—namely the Church. Paul's letters reveal that the Church, composed of both believing Jews and Gentiles, is the mystical body of Christ and all its members one in Him, a "mystery which from the beginning of the ages hath been hidden in God" (Eph. 3:9; cp. Mt. 13:11, 16–17, 34–35; 16:18). See *note* at Eph. 3:6; cp. *notes* at Mt. 13:11, 17; 16:18. It is in these same Epistles that the order, position, and duties of the Church are detailed. See The Epistles of Paul, NSRB, p. 1209. Paul emphasizes the doctrine of grace in salvation more than any other N.T. writer. Above all, the Pauline writings bear witness to the Person of Christ, His work and its meaning, and call upon Christians to live in a way that is worthy of their high calling in Christ.

2. The Epistle to the Hebrews, thought by some to be the work of Paul although his authorship cannot be proved, presents a clearer picture of the present ministry of the ascended Christ in heaven than any other book in the Bible. It contains a series of contrasts between the old things of Judaism and the superior things that the Christian possesses in Christ. See NSRB, p. 1311, the introduction to Hebrews.

3. The General Epistles, written by James, Peter, John, and Jude, relate to Paul's Epistles somewhat as John's Gospel bears upon the Synoptics. They round out N.T. teaching by supplementing what has already been stated in Paul's writings. See The General Epistles, NSRB, p. 1326.

d. The Revelation

Generally called The Revelation of St. John the Divine, the last book of the Bible is in reality "the revelation of Jesus Christ," as its first sentence states. It is the book of last things. It records what its writer, the Apostle John, saw and heard when he was a prisoner on the Isle of Patmos on account of his testimony for the Lord Jesus Christ (1:9–10). Some think that The Revelation cannot be understood, that it is a book of hidden things, whereas its very title (translated from the Greek word *apokálypsis*, which means *unveiling*) suggests the contrary. This revelation was given to John "to show unto [Christ's] servants things which must shortly come to pass" (1:1), things to be made known by signs and symbols. A special blessing is pronounced upon those who heed its words (1:3).

The Revelation tells of the consummation of all things in Christ. As the history of man begins in a garden where he fell (Gen. 2:8—3:7), so man's history ends by the river of the water of life beside the leaves of the tree of life, where the redeemed are healed for evermore to serve God and reign with Christ (22:1-5). This will take place following Christ's second advent and His millennial reign. Meanwhile, the very last words of the ascended Lord are written at the end of the book: "Surely, I come quickly." See NSRB, p. 1351, the introduction to The Revelation.

CHAPTER II

The Inspiration of the Scriptures

THE central facts of the Christian faith are the incarnation and the deity of Christ, His vicarious death on the cross for the atonement of sin, and His bodily resurrection from the dead. But essential to the faith is the inspiration of the Scriptures in which these facts are recorded. If the Bible is only the work of men and not the Word of God, then it is subject to human error and therefore fallible. If, on the other hand, the Bible is God's inspired Word, it is inerrant and a trustworthy record of God's revelation to man.

1. *What Inspiration Is*

As has already been stated,* about forty different men wrote the Bible over a period of approximately 1500 years. God the Holy Spirit inspired their writings, so that what these men wrote was without error in the original documents. See 1 Cor. 2:13, *note*. It was not only a part of Scripture but all of it that was given by inspiration of God (2 Tim. 3:16–17). The writers spoke "as they were moved by the Holy Spirit" (2 Pet. 1:21).

The doctrine of inspiration may be stated in this way: *The Bible, composed of all the books of the Old and New Testaments, is the Word of God which, written under the guidance of the Holy Spirit by human instruments whose intelligence, individuality, and literary style were not impaired, is the exact expression of God and, as such, was wholly without error in the original manuscripts.* What the Bible says, God says, for it is His Word. See 2 Tim. 3:16, *note*.

*Ch. I, p. 10.

2. *Some Internal Evidence of Inspiration*

Evidences of divine inspiration abound within the pages of the Bible, both in the Old Testament and the New Testament. Again and again such expressions as "thus saith the Lord" and "it is written" occur. Other self-claims to inspiration are made throughout the Scriptures, for example the O.T.'s ascription to the sanctifying power of God's judgments, laws, statutes, and words, and the N.T.'s insistence that the O.T. is God's Word to men. The N.T. also claims inspiration for itself (2 Tim. 3:16; cp. 2 Pet. 3:15–16).

A. Fulfilled Prophecy

One of the most convincing testimonies to the inspiration of the Scriptures is the fulfillment of Bible prophecy. See 2 Pet. 1:19, *note*. As a point of illustration more than twenty O.T. predictions relating to events that would surround the death of Christ, words written centuries before His first advent, were fulfilled with precision within a twenty-four-hour period at the time of His crucifixion. For example in Matthew 27:35 it is written, "And they crucified him, and parted his garments, casting lots." This was in fulfillment of Psalm 22:18, where it is stated, "They part my garments among them, and cast lots upon my vesture."

The Roman soldiers knew nothing of the O.T., of a Messianic Psalm predicting the Messiah's death. See Ps. 118:29, *note*. It was not to fulfill Psalm 22 (where see *notes*) that these men cast lots for our Lord's clothing but because they wanted to do so. Their act was ordained and controlled by God in order that His Word would not fail and to give evidence to His chosen people that it was indeed their Messiah who hung upon the cross.

For other prophecies fulfilled at the same time compare Mt. 26:21–25 with Ps. 41:9; Mt. 26:31, 56, Mk. 14:50 with Zech. 13:7; Mt. 26:59 with Ps. 35:11; Mt. 26:63, 27:12, 14, Mk. 14:61 with Isa. 53:7; Mt. 26:67 with Isa. 50:6, 52:14, Mic. 5:1, Zech. 13:7; Mt. 27:9 with Zech. 11:12–13; Mt. 27:27 with Isa. 53:8; Mt. 27:34, Mk. 15:36, Jn. 19:29 with Ps. 69:21; Mt. 27:38,

Mk. 15:27–28, Lk. 22:37, 23:32 with Isa. 53:12; Mt. 27:46, Mk. 15:34 with Ps. 22:1; Mt. 27:60, Mk. 15:46, Lk. 23:53, Jn. 19:41 with Isa. 53:9; Lk. 23:34 with Isa. 53:12; Jn. 19:28 with Ps. 69:21; Jn. 19:33, 36 with Ps. 34:20; Jn. 19:34, 37 with Zech. 12:10.

Fulfilled prophecy may also be traced in another way. In Matthew's Gospel alone there are sixteen places where it is stated that such and such an event occurred in fulfillment of an O.T. prophecy or so that an O.T. prophecy might be fulfilled (Mt. 1:22; 2:5, 15, 17, 23; 3:3; 4:14; 8:17; 11:10; 12:17; 13:14; 15:7; 21:4; 26:56; 27:9, 35).

B. Old Testament Evidences

"Thus saith the Lord," "the Lord said to Moses," "the Lord spoke, saying," and like expressions occur over and over again in the O.T. Exodus 24:4 reads, "Moses wrote all the words of the Lord." The first verse of the Book of Joshua states, "Now . . . the Lord spoke unto Joshua." See also Ex. 20:1; Lev. 1:1; Dt. 5:4; 2 Sam. 23:2–3; Isa. 59:21; Jer. 1:9. Our Lord affirmed the inspiration of the O.T. (Lk. 24:25–27; cp. Mt. 5:18; 22:42–44; Mk. 12:36; Jn. 10:35), as did the apostles (Acts 1:16; 4:24–26; 28:25–27; Heb. 1:1; 3:7–11; 10:15–17; 2 Pet. 1:20–21). Most convincing is Christ's own use of the O.T. Scriptures in His own life, e.g. at His temptation (Mt. 4:4, 7, 10), and as applying to Himself in their testimony (Jn. 5:39). Thus we stand with Him when it comes to the trustworthiness of the Old Testament.

C. New Testament Evidences

Christ Himself gave pre-authentication of the inspiration of the N.T. See Jn. 16:12, *note*. He promised that He had many things to say to His followers and that these things would be revealed after the advent of the Holy Spirit, who would teach them all about them (Jn. 16:12–15; cp. Jn. 14:26). There is clear intimation that what He spoke about would be recorded for the Church (Mt. 10:14–15; 28:19; Lk. 10:16; Jn. 13:20; 15:20, 27;

17:20; Acts 1:8; also Rom. 16:25–27; Eph. 3:3–5; 4:11–12). The apostles affirmed that their writings in the N.T. were inspired (1 Cor. 2:13; 14:37; Gal. 1:6–9; 1 Th. 4:2, 15; 2 Th. 3:6, 12, 14; 2 Pet. 3:15–16).

D. The Unity of the Bible

The unity of the Bible, most of its sixty-six books being written independently of the others and yet harmonizing with them to make a perfect pattern, is evidence of its inspiration. Let any other group of about two score writers produce over a period of a millennium and a half a volume of sixty-six books that form a unity, books by which men can live and die. Only by divine inspiration could such a thing be done.

3. *Some External Indications of Inspiration*

A book may be trustworthy without being inspired. For instance, an English grammar will almost certainly stress a rule of syntax—that a sentence having a singular subject requires a singular verb. This is a fact but not divinely inspired truth. Two plus two equals four is a trustworthy equation, but a book on mathematics does not claim inspiration for itself. On the other hand, a book that is not trustworthy cannot be divinely inspired. God is the God of truth and an untrustworthy book would be incompatible with His nature.

Archaeology is one of the major illustrations of the trust-worthiness of the Bible. Deity does not require from humanity or the physical world testimony concerning divine reliability. Let the skeptics take note, however, that over the years find after find has been unearthed in Bible lands that bears witness to the unfailing accuracy and trustworthiness of the Scriptures. See e.g. *notes* at 2 Ki. 7:6; 2 Chr. 8:17.

External illumination of the accuracy of the Bible and the reliability of its historicity, however, are not proof of its inspiration. Rather, he who reads it in faith and with receptivity discovers that there is an inward witness of the Holy Spirit that assures him that this Book is indeed the inspired Word of God.

Among the strongest external indications that the Bible is "God-breathed" (2 Tim. 3:16, *lit.*) is its effect upon the lives of men. What other book has changed social outcasts and enemies of the cross of Christ into men and women of godly character? What other book brings to its readers life, and peace, and satisfaction, and joy? What other book can serve as spiritual food to hungry hearts day after day, year after year, decade after decade? The Bible never wears out. It remains always fresh and edifying. It never fails and is changeless (Lk. 16:17; 1 Pet. 1:23, 25). It brings men close to God and keeps them there. One may not understand some of the things that are written in the Bible, but he can believe all of it (cp. Rom. 10:17).

Above all, the supreme argument for inspiration is that Christ trusted implicitly the Scriptures of His time, the O.T. Indeed, He often seemed to go out of His way to confirm historical facts that are denied today in many places, facts such as the flood, Lot's wife, and Jonah and the great fish (Mt. 12:40–41; 24:37–39; Lk. 17:32).

4. *Some Common Questions*

Certain questions have been raised about the inspiration of the Scriptures.

(a) Were the men who wrote the books of the O.T. and the N.T. no more than automata who acted in an involuntary and mechanical way in which their human personalities, talents, and knowledge had no part? Were they like stenographers taking down dictation? Not at all. God made use of their personalities, emotions, intelligence, and literary style in such a way that they recorded, by the governance of the Holy Spirit, an accurate revelation of the message God wished them to convey.

(b) If the original documents of Scripture were inspired by God the Holy Spirit so as to be without error, why did He not govern the copies made from these manuscripts, so that they, too, would be without error? We do not know. God's thoughts and ways are not our thoughts and ways (Isa. 55:8–9). But is it not remarkable that there were so few mistakes in copying the ancient manuscripts in contrast with the innumerable facts that are obviously true and accurate? And none of these "mistakes" affects the vital messages of the Bible concerning God, and man's relationship to Him. Furthermore, since all the facts relating to the Scriptures may not yet be fully known, it is not entirely out of order to suggest that no one really has sufficient information to prove an error in the Bible.

(c) What about the contradictions in the Bible? The burden of proof that there are discrepancies lies with those who pose the question. There are some inconsistencies in numbers in available texts. But these are undoubtedly the result of copyists' mistakes. There are no contradictions concerning faith and life. See *notes* at 1 Sam. 6:19; 1 Chr. 11:11. When Scripture is compared with Scripture most alleged contradictions, other than scribal errors, disappear. As for the comparatively few to which there seems at present to be no answer, an attitude of faith manifested in suspended judgment is indicated. For already many seeming discrepancies regarding the Bible have been reconciled as further knowledge has come to light.

He who reads the Bible prayerfully, thoughtfully, and receptively will discover for himself, as have innumerable others before him, that it is indeed the Word of God and is profitable for teaching, for conviction, for correction, and for instruction in righteousness (cp. 2 Tim. 3:16).

CHAPTER III

God

GOD is one. "Hear, O Israel: The LORD our God is one LORD" (Dt. 6:4). "Thus saith the LORD, the King of Israel, and his redeemer, the LORD of hosts: I am the first, and I am the last, and beside me there is no God" (Isa. 44:6).

Yet that the one God subsisted in three Persons—the Father, the Son, and the Holy Spirit—is intimated in the Old Testament and substantiated in the New Testament. Christ's disciples were commanded to go and teach all nations, "baptizing them in the name [*singular noun*] of the Father, and of the Son, and of the Holy Spirit" (Mt. 28:19), and the church at Corinth was blessed by the Apostle Paul in these words: "The grace of the Lord Jesus Christ, and the love of God, and the communion of the Holy Spirit be with you all" (2 Cor. 13:14). Cp. 1 Cor. 12:4–6; Eph. 4:4–6; 1 Pet. 1:2; Jude 20–21.

The triune Being of the Godhead, one God in three Persons, is a mystery beyond explanation, in truth beyond comprehension. But it is a fact of divine revelation and Christians accept it by faith. In essence God is one; in His Persons God is three. The divine Essence cannot be divided; the divine Persons must be distinguished. See Mt. 28:19, *note.*

1. *The Plurality of the Godhead*

The divine plurality is revealed in the first sentence of the Bible: "In the beginning God created the heaven and the earth." The Hebrew word for "God" in this sentence is *Elohim* (*'elôhîm*), in form a plural noun. At the same time the oneness of God is also asserted. For although a plural noun, when it is the subject of a sentence or clause, requires a plural verb, here the verb "created" (from the Hebrew bārāʼ) is in the singular number. God is one. Yet God is more than one. Compare Genesis 1:26, "And God said, Let us make man in our image, after our likeness," with verse 27, "So God created man in his own image." See Gen. 1:1, *note 3*.

2. *The Godhead Is Composed of Three Persons*

The plurality of God involves not two but three Persons,* each of them no less God than the others, each having the same glory, attributes, and power. As an illustration, the creation of the universe is attributed to three Persons—the Father, the Son, and the Holy Spirit. Of God the Father it is written, "O my God . . . of old hast thou laid the foundations of the earth; and the heavens are the work of thy hands" (Ps. 102:24–25). Of God the Son it is said, "For by him were all things created, that are in heaven, and that are in earth, visible and invisible" (Col. 1:16). And of God the Holy Spirit it is stated, "By his Spirit he hath garnished the heavens" (Job 26:13) and "Thou sendest forth thy Spirit, they are created; and thou renewest the face of the earth" (Ps. 104:30). Compare also the creation account of Genesis 1: "And the Spirit of God moved upon the face of the waters" (v. 2).

The N.T. more than once affirms the fact of the Holy Trinity, although the word "trinity" is never used in the Bible. When John the Baptist baptized Jesus at the outset of His ministry, as Jesus came up out of the water the Holy Spirit was visible, hovering over Him like a dove and lighting upon Him. The Father spoke from heaven, saying, "This is my beloved Son, in whom I am well pleased" (Mt. 3:16–17). In this same Gospel, when at the conclusion of Christ's earthly ministry He gave His commission to the eleven apostles, He told them, as has already been mentioned, to

---

*It is of interest to observe that whereas in the Hebrew language there are three numbers—singular, dual, and plural—the name "God" has no dual but only singular and plural.

go to all nations, "baptizing them in the name of the Father, and of the Son, and of the Holy Spirit" (Mt. 28:19).

Furthermore, the blending of the names and the work of the Father, the Son, and the Holy Spirit in the Apostle John's first letter give evidence that the one true God has three distinct personalities: "No man hath seen God at any time. If we love one another, God dwelleth in us, and his love is perfected in us. By this we know that we dwell in him, and he in us, because he hath given us of his Spirit. And we have seen and do testify that the Father sent the Son to be the Saviour of the world. Whosoever shall confess that Jesus is the Son of God, God dwelleth in him, and he in God. . . . This is he that came by water and blood, even Jesus Christ; not by water only, but by water and blood. And it is the Spirit that beareth witness, because the Spirit is truth. And there are three that bear witness in earth, the Spirit, and the water, and the blood; and these three agree in one. If we receive the witness of men, the witness of God is greater; for this is the witness of God which he hath testified of his Son. He that believeth on the Son of God hath the witness in himself. . . . And this is the record [that God gave of his Son], that God hath given to us eternal life, and this life is in his Son" (1 Jn. 4:12–15; 5:6–11).

3. *The Relationships and Functions of the Trinity*

Although the three Persons of the Godhead are distinct from one another, they are not independent of each other but are related and co-equal. The Father gives the Son (Isa. 9:6; Jn. 3:16) who, insofar as His perfect humanity is concerned, is conceived by the Holy Spirit (Mt. 1:18, 20; Lk. 1:35). The Holy Spirit proceeds from the Father (Jn. 14:16–17) and also from the Son (Jn. 16:7). The Spirit glorifies the Son (Jn. 16:14), the Son glorifies the Father (Jn. 17:4), and the Father glorifies the Son (Jn. 17:5). The Father has always been the Father, the Son has always been the Son, the Holy Spirit has always been the Holy Spirit. God the Father did not cease to exist when God the Son left heaven and came to earth to become a sacrifice for sin. God the Son is now seated at the Father's right hand as a distinct personality. God the Spirit is still God, though presently He is an abiding Presence within believers in Christ. Each of the three is God. To each of them—the Father, the Son, and the Spirit—the name "God" is applied (Gal. 1:1; Jn. 1:1; Acts 5:3-4).

The very fact that the Holy Trinity is a divine unity presupposes co-equality. When the Lord Jesus said to the Jews who opposed Him, "My Father worketh hitherto, and I work," they endeavored to kill Him because He said "that God was his father, making himself equal with God" (Jn. 5:17-18; cp. 10:30). And elsewhere in Scripture it is declared that in His eternal state Christ, the Son of God, was "in the form of God, [and that he] thought it not robbery [a thing to be held on to] to be equal with God" (Phil. 2:6). He is God in His own right.

When the same power, the same works, the same thoughts, and the same glory are attributed to the three Persons of the Godhead, co-equality must be ascribed to them. Earlier in this chapter it was shown from Scripture that the creation was the work of the Father, and of the Son, and of the Holy Spirit. The same is true of Christ's resurrection. Concerning the Father it is written, "Whom [Jesus of Nazareth] God raised up, having loosed the pains of death, because it was not possible that he should be held by it" (Acts 2:24; cp. Eph. 1:17, 19-20). Jesus claimed for Himself authority to rise from the dead, "I have power [*lit.* authority] to lay it [my life] down, and I have power [authority] to take it again" (Jn. 10:18; cp. 2:19-22). And concerning the Holy Spirit's part in Christ's resurrection, Peter declares, "For Christ also hath once suffered for sins, the just for the unjust, that he might bring us to God, being put to death in the flesh, but made alive by the Spirit" (1 Pet. 3:18).

Attributes that can belong only to deity are shared equally by the Godhead: eternal Being—God the Father (Ps. 90:1-4; Isa. 40:28), God the Son (Mic. 5:2; Jn. 8:58), and God the Holy Spirit (Heb. 9:14); omniscience—the Father (Ps. 147:5; 1 Jn. 3:20), the Son (Jn. 16:30; Col. 2:3), although in His humanity

He may limit the extent of His knowledge (Mk. 13:32), and the Spirit (Jn. 14:26; I Cor. 2:10–11); omnipotence—the Father (Gen. 18:14; Job 42:2), the Son (Mt. 28:18; Heb. 1:3), and the Spirit (Mic. 3:8; Zech. 4:6); omnipresence—the Father (Jer. 23:23–24), the Son (Mt. 18:20), and the Spirit (Ps. 139:7–10). Other attributes shared by the Father, the Son, and the Holy Spirit include goodness, holiness, justice, love, power, and a disposition for fellowship. See Rom. 1:18, *note*.

A. GOD THE FATHER

Each person of the Trinity is characterized by specific properties and ministries, some of which coincide, since the three Persons of the Godhead compose the one true God. For example God the Father is manifested especially in heaven through His glory (Dt. 5:24; I Ki. 8:11; Ps. 19:1; Isa. 42:8), His holiness (Isa. 5:16; I Pet. 1:15–16), His righteousness (Ezra 9:15), His mercy (Ps. 103:8), His grace (Ps. 145:8; Rom. 3:23–24), His faithfulness (Dt. 7:9; I Cor. 10:13; 2 Tim. 2:13; I Jn. 1:9), His love (Jer. 31:3; Jn. 3:16; see Dt. 6:5, *note*), and as a prayer-answering Father (Jn. 11:22; 16:23; Phil. 4:6–7) and the Supplier of all our needs (Phil. 4:19).

B. GOD THE SON

God the Son is manifested particularly in His redemptive work on earth and present ministry in heaven, as the sinless and Holy One (2 Cor. 5:21; Heb. 7:26; I Pet. 2:22), the suffering Servant (Isa. 52:13, where see *note*), Redeemer (I Pet. 1:18–19), Reconciler (2 Cor. 5:19), Mediator (I Tim. 2:5–6), Shepherd (Jn. 10:11, 17–30; see Jn. 10:7, *note*), Strengthener (Phil. 4:13), Intercessor (Heb. 7:25), Advocate (I Jn. 2:1–2), and Heir of all things (Heb. 1:2), a Lord of grace (2 Cor. 8:9) whose love of mankind and His Church is limitless (Eph. 3:19; 5:25). The Son of God is the visible image of the invisible God (Col. 1:15: Heb. 1:3). See Jn. 1:18, *note*.

C. GOD THE HOLY SPIRIT

God the Holy Spirit is manifested peculiarly as the One who dwells within believers in Christ (1 Cor. 6:19) and, as an abiding Presence, encourages and comforts them (Jn. 14:16), empowers and guards them (1 Cor. 3:16; Eph. 4:30; Phil. 1:6), bestows spiritual gifts (1 Cor. 12:4-11; see Eph. 4:11, *notes*), gives victory over the flesh (Rom. 8:4-5, 13; Gal. 5:16-17), and as the divine agent who touches hearts and convicts men of sin, of righteousness, and of judgment (Jn. 16:7-11). See *notes* at Zech. 12:10; Acts 2:4.

God the Father is very God of very God. God the Son is very God of very God. And who is the Son? Jesus Christ (Jn. 1:1, 14; 20:31), whose deity is both intimated and explicitly predicted in the O.T. and affirmed many times in the N.T. See *notes* at Jn. 20:28; Acts. 9:20; Phil. 2:6; Jas. 2:1. God the Spirit is very God of very God, proceeding from the Father and the Son.

CHAPTER IV

Angels

THE word "angel" in its various forms appears over 250 times in the English Bible. The Hebrew noun is *mal'âk,* the Greek word, *ággelos* (pronounced anǧĕlŏs). The literal meaning of both words is *messenger*. An angel is a messenger.

With rare exceptions, angels in Scripture are supernatural beings, most of them messengers of God but some of them agents of Satan. Their number is great (Heb. 12:22; Rev. 5:11). Their power is awesome (e.g. 2 Ki. 19:35).

Angels are created beings (Col. 1:16). They are always referred to in the masculine gender. While upon occasion they inhabit material bodies that resemble men (e.g. Acts 1:10; Heb. 13:2), they are spirits (Heb. 1:14). There are such things as spiritual bodies (cp. 2 Ki. 6:15–17), but these would be invisible to the human eye. See Heb. 1:4, *note.*

There are government, authority, and power among the angelic beings. In Colossians 1:16, some of the objects of Christ's creative power are said to be "thrones, or dominions, or principalities, or powers." Elsewhere in Scripture, where allusion is made to Satan before his fall, he is spoken of as "the anointed cherub that covereth" (Ezek. 28:14), whom God placed in that office. See Ezek. 28:12, *note.* Michael is called "the archangel" (Jude 9), a title that implies primacy.

There are two exceptions to this general classification of angels:

(a) The Bible speaks of a particular angel who surpasses all angelic beings in kind and degree—the angel of the Lord. He is called "the angel of the Lord" (e.g. Gen. 16:7), "the angel of God" (e.g. Gen. 21:17), and "the angel of his [God's] presence" (Isa. 63:9). See Jud. 2:1, *note* on pp. 289–90.

The angel of the Lord is not a created being but the Creator Himself, the second Person of the Godhead, the eternal Son who, before His incarnation, manifested Himself in various forms, sometimes as a man, e.g. He spoke to Moses out of a flame of fire and appeared in corporeal form to Balaam (Ex. 3:2; Num. 22:31, see vv. 22–35). His appearances in human form are known as theophanies, from a Greek noun meaning *God manifested*. See Gen. 12:7, *note* 1.

As the angel of the Lord, the Son of God was higher than the angels but in His humanity He was made lower than the angels for a little time (Ps. 8:5–6; Heb. 2:7–8). Now He has been made superior to the angels and is crowned with glory and honor (Heb. 1:4; 2:7). Always He has been worshiped by them (Heb. 1:6).

The New Testament refers to angels as from God but makes no reference to *the* angel of the Lord for the obvious reason that, beginning with the Son's incarnation and until His ascent into heaven, God was dwelling among men in fashion as a man (Jn. 1:14; Phil. 2:6–8).*

(b) In Revelation 2 and 3 the messengers to the seven churches are referred to as angels, e.g. "the angel of the church of Ephesus" (Rev. 2:1). From the context it is evident that these angels are men, not supernatural beings. See Rev. 1:20, *note* 3.

1. *Holy Angels*

The holy angels fall into various categories:

(a) There are those who are called "elect angels" (1 Tim. 5:21). It is not clear whether they compose all the holy angels or whether they are a select group among them. The former is perhaps true, just as all believers in Christ are spoken of as being elect (e.g. Ti. 1:1; 1 Pet. 1:2).

(b) There are the cherubim, who are mentioned more than eighty times in the Bible (e.g. 1 Sam. 4:4; Ps. 80:1). Lucifer,

---

*In the KJV at Matthew 1:20; 2:13; 28:2; Luke 2:9; Acts 5:19; 8:26; 12:7; 27:23 the definite article is used in error. This is corrected in the NSRB.

"the anointed cherub," was doubtless of their number before he became Satan (meaning *adversary*) through his fall. The cherubim are first alluded to as guardians of the gate of Eden (Gen. 3:24). They are portrayed by figures of gold on the mercy seat of the ark of the covenant (Ex. 25:19).

(c) There are the seraphim (Isa. 6:2), whose ministry appears to be that of worshiping and praising God continually as they cry one to another, "Holy, holy, holy, is the LORD of hosts; the whole earth is full of his glory" (v. 3).

(d) Another group of angelic beings, called "living creatures (KJV "beasts") in Revelation, may be identical with the seraphim of Isaiah 6, since they also are described as having six wings and offering praise to God, saying, "Holy, holy, holy, Lord God Almighty" (Rev. 4:8; cp. Isa. 6:2–3).

(e) Besides these, there is "an innumerable company of angels" (Heb. 12:22) concerning whom no special ministry is denoted.

The holy angels were witnesses of the epochal events of creation and of man's redemption. They are "the morning stars [who] sang together," "the sons of God [who] shouted for joy" when the foundations of the earth were laid (Job 38:4, 7). They were at hand when Jesus was born (Lk. 2:13–14), served Him when He was tempted by the devil (Mt. 4:11) and during His agony in Gethsemane (Lk. 22:43). They were Christ's attendants at the time of His resurrection and ascension (Jn. 20:12; Acts 1:10–11). The Lord Jesus Christ will be accompanied by all the holy angels when He returns to the earth in power and glory (Mt. 25:31).

The holy angels have been messengers of God since time immemorial (e.g. Gen. 19:1; Num. 20:16; Dan. 9:21; Mt. 1:20; Acts 5:19). Today, as in former times, they act as servants of God, "ministering spirits sent forth to minister for them who shall be heirs of salvation" (Heb. 1:14; cp. Ps. 34:7; Mt. 18:10).

From Genesis to Revelation, indeed from eternity to eternity, the holy angels render worship, praise, and adoration to the triune God. Thus the psalmist writes: "Praise ye the LORD. . . .

Praise ye him, all his angels. . . . Praise ye him, sun and moon; praise ye him, all ye stars of light" (Ps. 148:1–3).

Only two of the holy angels are identified by name in the Scriptures—Gabriel and Michael. Gabriel, whose name means *man of God* or *God has shown Himself strong*, is a courier of God to deliver unusually important messages. He was sent to Daniel to interpret his visions to him (Dan. 8:15–19; 9:20–23), visions which unfolded the divine program concerning certain activities of the Jews and the Gentiles for centuries to come. Gabriel was also God's messenger to bring to Zacharias, a temple priest at Jerusalem, the news that Zacharias and Elisabeth his wife were to have a son, John the Baptist, in their old age (Lk. 1:11–20, 60, 63). Gabriel announced to Mary, a virgin of Nazareth, that she would have a son, Jesus, who would be called "the Son of the Highest" (Lk. 1:26–33).

Michael is identified in Daniel 10:13, 21 as a prince, and in Jude 9 as the archangel. His name means *who is like God.* He is an angel of war, the commander-in-chief of the angels who battle against Satan and his hosts. Michael assisted one of the holy angels, perhaps Gabriel, in the latter's encounter with a wicked angel identified as the prince of Persia (Dan. 10:20–21). Michael disputed with the devil about the body of Moses (Jude 9) and will fight against Satan and his angels in a future war in heaven (Rev. 12:7–9).

Michael has a particular relationship with Israel. He is spoken of as "Michael, your [Daniel's] prince" (Dan. 10:21) and as "the great prince who standeth for the children of thy [Daniel's] people" (Dan. 12:1). This will be at a period when Israel as a nation will suffer "a time of trouble, such as never was since there was a nation even to that same time"—that is, during the great tribulation predicted by Christ in His Olivet Discourse (Mt. 24:21ff.). It is in relation to Israel too that Michael will contend with Satan, a matter that has already been mentioned (Rev. 12:7–9).

Michael is the only archangel named by name. But his identification as "one of the chief princes" (Dan. 10:13) implies that there may be other archangels. It is generally assumed, however, that it will be Michael's voice which will be heard when the

Lord Jesus comes to translate His Church to heaven (1 Th. 4:16–17). As important and powerful as Michael is, however, there is another angelic being, Satan,* whom the archangel cannot fight alone nor accuse before God. For in his controversy with Satan concerning Moses' body, it is recorded that he "dared not bring against him [the devil] a railing accusation, but said, The Lord rebuke thee" (Jude 9).

2. *Wicked Angels*

God alone has the power to create. All things that He made were good. It must be inferred, therefore, that the existence of wicked angels comes from Satan's rebellion against God. When he said, "I will ascend into heaven, I will exalt my throne above the stars of God. . . . I will be like the Most High" (Isa. 14:12–14, where see *note* at v. 12), a band of angels rebelled with him. The wicked angels fell from their high office as messengers of God and became emissaries of the devil. The fallen angels fit into two categories—those who are imprisoned and those who are free.

(a) Already judgment has been passed upon the angels who are imprisoned, although their final punishment is still future. It is written concerning them that "God spared not the angels that sinned, but cast them down to hell [translated from the Greek word *tartaröö*, which relates to a place comparable to hades], and delivered them into chains of darkness, to be reserved unto judgment" (2 Pet. 2:4). And Jude says that "the angels who kept not their first estate, but left their own habitation, he hath reserved in everlasting chains under darkness unto the judgment of the great day" (Jude 6, where see *note*).† See Heb. 1:4, *note* (last par. p. 1312).

*See Ch. V.

†It has not been revealed just what the specific sin was that caused this particular group of angels to be imprisoned. Certainly all the fallen angels had at one time joined with Satan in his rebellion. Jude's expression, "kept not their first estate," may provide the clue and, as some Bible students think, Genesis 6:1–2 the solution.

(b) Other fallen angels are at liberty and are active. They go about doing the will of Satan. Their work is to try to corrupt the world system and to defeat Christians. They comprise, with Satan their leader, the principalities, powers, and rulers of this world's darkness (Eph. 6:12). They form Satan's well-ordered kingdom to which our Lord solemnly referred (Mt. 12:25–29).

Some of the wicked angels are designated as seducing spirits (1 Tim. 4:1, where see *note*). Others are spoken of as demons* or dumb spirits or unclean spirits, spirit beings that need to inhabit bodies that are either human or bestial (e.g. Mt. 8:28–34; Mk. 5:2; 9:17).

The final judgment of all fallen angels will take place when Satan's sentence is executed (Mt. 25:41; Rev. 20:10).

Only one of the fallen angels is called by name in Scripture. His original name was Lucifer (Isa. 14:12). He is better known as Satan (e.g. 1 Chr. 21:1; Job 1:6; Ps. 109:6; Zech. 3:1; Mt. 4:10; Jn. 13:27; Rom. 16:20; Rev. 12:9) or the devil (e.g. Mt. 4:1; Jn. 8:44; Acts 10:38; Eph. 6:11; Heb. 2:14; 1 Pet. 5:8). Lucifer was created the highest of the angels, "full of wisdom, and perfect in beauty . . . till iniquity was found in [him]" (Ezek. 28:12, 15).

Two other wicked angels are identified, not by name but by title or realm of authority—the prince of the kingdom of Persia, who withstood God's angelic messenger to Daniel, and the prince of Greece (Dan. 10:13, 20)—from which it may be inferred that Satan appoints mighty angels in an effort to influence rulers to do his will rather than God's will.

Angels, then, are spirit beings. Some of them are holy and serve God in accordance with His will. Others are wicked and serve Satan, their prince. Redeemed men and women are now a little lower than the angels; in this respect they are on a plateau with the Son of God in His incarnation, when He was made lower than the angels for a little time (Heb. 2:7, 9). As He is higher than

---

*In the KJV the word "devils" is used. There is only one devil, Satan (Gk. *diábolos*). There are many demons (Gk. pl. *daimónia*). To render *daimónia* "devils" in Matthew 4:24; 7:22, where see *note*; 8:16; etc. is incorrect.

the angels now (v. 8), so believers in Him will one day be higher than they, although they will never be worshiped by the angels as He is (Heb. 1:6), for only deity may be worshiped.

CHAPTER V

Satan

T HE highest of God's creatures is the angelic being Lucifer, who fell through pride and became Satan. His other names and designations are the anointed cherub, the devil, the prince of this world, the evil one, the prince of the power of the air, the tempter, that wicked one, the dragon, and the serpent (1 Chr. 21:1; Isa. 14:12; Ezek. 28:14; Mt. 4:1; Jn. 12:31; 17:15, *marg.*; Eph. 2:2; 1 Th. 3:5; 1 Jn. 5:18; Rev. 12:7, 9).

There is wide misconception of the personality, appearance, and dwelling place of Satan. This stems from ignorance concerning what the Bible says about him and from the influence of folklore and secular writings. On the one hand, he is stripped of personality and spoken of as merely the spirit of evil; on the other hand, he is assumed to be the ruler of hell, which is thought to be his habitation. Cartoons portray him as a grotesque creature, part man and part beast, having horns, hooves, and a spiked tail, who is usually pictured prodding hell's inhabitants with a pitchfork. While Satan is a spirit and is the great protagonist of evil, nothing could be further from the truth than these caricatures. For not only is Satan not the ruler of hell; he has never been in hell at all. On the contrary, he is perhaps the most beautiful of God's creatures. His realm is the heavens; indeed he has access to heaven itself (Job 1:6; 2:1).

1. *Satan's History*

Satan's creation took place before time, as we know it, began—perhaps in the mysterious period prior to Genesis 1:1. He was doubtless created as one of the cherubim (see Ezek. 1:5, *note*), since he is called "the anointed cherub that covereth" in a passage which, although it is addressed to the prince of Tyre, is written in language that goes beyond him to the unseen ruler of the world system (Ezek. 28:11–15). See *notes* at Ezek. 28:12; Rev. 13:8. He was originally perfect in wisdom and beauty, as Ezekiel says. But his heart was lifted up against God and iniquity was found in him because of his pride, which is exemplified by his declaration, "I will be like the Most High" (Isa. 14:13–14). When Lucifer fell, sin entered the universe. See Isa. 14:12, *note*.

"Eden, the garden of God" (Ezek. 28:13), a place filled with precious stones and apparently not the Eden of Genesis 1 and 2, seems to have been Satan's dwelling place before his fall.

2. *Satan's Present Activities*

Since his fall, the devil's purpose has not changed—to be like the Most High and to draw worship away from God and to himself. His present spheres of activity are in the air and on the earth (Eph. 2:2; 1 Pet. 5:8). A liar from the beginning (Jn. 8:44), his first act after man's creation was to seduce Eve by his craftiness (2 Cor. 11:3), approaching her in the guise of a serpent and influencing her to doubt the wisdom and power of God. See Gen. 3:1, *note*. This brought about Adam's downfall also and, through Adam, the ruin of the rest of mankind. In this way the supernatural being who introduced sin into the universe was responsible for the origin of sin in the world of men (Rom. 5:12–14).

Ever since he enticed Eve to sin in the Genesis Eden, Satan has been turning men and women away from God and testing those who are God's faithful people (Job 1:6–11; Lk. 22:31). The present world system, of which he is the unseen ruler (Jn. 14:30) and in which force, selfishness, and greed reign, is his masterpiece. Its dominion is the prize he offered Jesus when he tempted Him in the wilderness (Mt. 4:8–9).

Satan's power is limited only by God, under whose permissive will he is able to debase mankind and topple kingdoms. Furthermore, he has power to cause sickness (Job 2:7) and do miraculous deeds (Job 1:16, 19). He was even given the power to bring death to men, but only with divine permission (Job 2:6; Heb. 2:14; cp. 1 Sam. 23:14).

Because he sometimes appears as "an angel of light" (2 Cor. 11:14–15), Satan, in whom there is no truth but only deception, deludes men through his agents into accepting false teaching as truth. No stronger condemnation of him could be made than what the Lord Jesus said, "He was a murderer from the beginning, and abode not in the truth, because there is no truth in him. When he speaketh a lie, he speaketh of his own; for he is a liar, and the father of it" (Jn. 8:44). The Christian must fight against such a deceiver and his demons (see Mt. 7:22, *note*), by putting on the whole armor of God in order to stand against the devil's stratagems (Eph. 6:10–18).

Satan continues to have access to God as the accuser of God's people, but in the end time this privilege will be retracted (Rev. 12:10).

3. *Satan's Doom*

When Satan was hurled down from the mountain of God, God told him that he would be destroyed and brought down to hell (Isa. 14:15; cp. Ezek. 28:16). When Christ was on earth He said that the prince of this world would be cast out (Jn. 12:31).

A series of events will bring about this everlasting doom. They will begin when the devil is cast out of heaven by Michael and his angels, a scene viewed by John on Patmos (Rev. 12:7–9). After the war at Armageddon (Rev. 19:17–21) and just before the millennium Satan will be bound and shut up in the abyss, which will be sealed for a thousand years (Rev. 20:1–3). Following this period he will be freed from the abyss for a time during which he will resume his deception of mankind and will be so successful that he will be able to gather multitudes to make war against "the beloved city" and all God's people on earth. But fire from heaven will destroy his armies, and he himself will be cast alive into the lake of fire, a place prepared long ago for him and his angels, where he will be judged forever (Rev. 20:7–10; cp. Mt. 25:41). See Rev. 20:10, *note*.

CHAPTER VI

Creation

V ERY few people have been able to escape asking themselves how the universe began. Where did everything come from? What was here before the earth was formed? If there is a God, where and when did He originate? These are reasonable questions which demand an answer.

God cannot be proved by human reason. He is made known by revelation. Man may have the intuition that there is a God or he may deduce that there must be a God, but he cannot prove his intuition or reasonings by his formal logic or by his scientific thinking. Nevertheless, God has not left mankind without evidences of His existence, such as the innumerable marks of design in the universe, from the harmony of the solar system to the wonders of life. But God can be truly known through revelation. He has spoken in His Word, the Bible. He has revealed Himself in His Son, who is His express image (Heb. 1:3; cp. Col. 1:15). The mature Christian accepts by faith what God has made known in the Scriptures (Heb. 11:3).

To the man of faith there is no conflict between true science and the Bible. When, therefore, science appears to contradict the Bible, one of two conclusions must be drawn: either science is in error or the Scriptures have been misinterpreted. For God is the God of all truth.

At the beginning of the Bible the origin of the universe is told in terms so simple as to be intelligible to the uneducated, yet so profound as to invite the attention of the most learned. For although the Bible is not a textbook on science or philosophy, what it reveals on these subjects is true. Man's theories about God and the universe cannot supplant the authority of God Himself.

1. *The Origin of the Universe*

God created the universe out of nothing. "In the beginning God"—not God and matter. "In the beginning God created the heavens and the earth." The heavens and the earth are composed of matter.

"In the beginning was the Word, and the Word was with God, and the Word was God. All things were made by him, and without him was not anything made that was made" (Jn. 1:1, 3). "For by him were all things created, that are in heaven and that are on earth, visible and invisible, whether they be thrones, or dominions, or principalities, or powers; all things were created by him and for him; and he is before all things, and by him all things consist" (Col. 1:16–17). By the Godhead all things visible and invisible were created. The sun, the moon, and the stars are visible, and by Him all things visible were created. The sun, the moon, and the stars are material. God created material things. He created them out of nothing. There was no substance prior to creation. God alone is eternal.

The mysteries as to God's Being and how He existed before He created the universe, and also how He brought the universe into existence, must remain mysteries. "In the beginning God . . ." We must leave it there. God is God.

2. *The Creation of the Earth*

The Genesis account of the earth's creation differs from all extra-biblical theories, in that God was its source. Moses could not have known from experience how the earth was formed, nor could Adam. Neither of them was there when it happened. Moses' record in Genesis was inspired by the Holy Spirit. Just as the veil was lifted from Daniel's eyes so that he could see into the future, so Moses was enabled by the Spirit of God to gaze backward and record primordial facts. As a holy man of God he spoke as he was moved by the Holy Spirit (2 Pet. 1:21).

In modern times both geologists and archaeologists have discovered evidences indicating that the earth has been in existence a very long time. But all that has been brought to light is in harmony with and not contradictory to the Scriptures.

The Bible begins with the beginnings: "In the beginning God created the heaven and the earth. And the earth was without form and void; and darkness was upon the face of the deep. And the Spirit of God moved upon the face of the waters. And God said, Let there be light; and there was light. And God saw the light, that it was good; and God divided the light from the darkness. And God called the light Day, and the darkness he called Night. And the evening and the morning were the first day" (Gen. 1:1-5).

No one knows the date of the earth's creation. See Gen. 1:1, note 2; cp. notes at Gen. 5:3; 11:10. Even the most conservative scholars are generally agreed that no date prior to about 2500 B.C. can be fixed accurately. The creation of the universe could have been many millions of years ago without contradicting Genesis 1:1. The creation of man could have been vastly earlier than 4000 B.C. without refuting the Bible. There could have been a span of innumerable years between what is recorded in verses 1 and 2 of Genesis 1, and countless years between the two sentences of verse 2.

Among biblical scholars there are two interpretations of the words "without form and void" in verse 2: (a) that the expression denotes the original formless condition of the earth in the first stage of its creation, and (b) that "without form and void" describes the condition of the earth subsequent to its original creation (perhaps as a result of judgment) and prior to the latter half of verse 2, "And the Spirit of God moved upon the face of the waters." The former view is generally known as the Original Chaos Interpretation, the latter as the Divine Judgment or Gap Interpretation. See notes at Gen. 1:3; Isa. 45:18. In either case there could have been a period of an indefinite number of years—billions if you wish—before God's Spirit moved upon the waters.

Were the six days of creation periods of twenty-four hours each or were they longer? That God, who is omniscient, could have formed the universe and everything in it in a flashing moment or in six twenty-four-hour days is not open to question. At the same time it should be kept in mind that the word "day" is used in the Bible in various ways. It is employed to denote (a) a period of twenty-four hours (Mt. 17:1); (b) that portion of the solar day during which it is light, in contrast with night (Jn. 11:9–10); (c) a time that is set apart for a specific purpose, e.g. "day of atonement" (Lev. 23:27); and (d) a longer period of time in which certain divine programs are carried out, e.g. "in the day when the LORD God made the earth and the heavens" (Gen. 2:4), or "day of visitation" (1 Pet. 2:12). See Gen. 1:5, *notes* on pp. 1 and 2. The days of creation might have been days of twenty-four hours each or they could have been aeons in duration. (Among earnest Christians both views are held.) In those six days God created light, the world in which we live, the heavenly bodies, vegetation, and all living creatures, of whom the highest is man.

3. *The Creation of Man*

There are two biblical accounts of man's creation: (1) a general statement in Genesis 1:26–27, and (2) a more detailed account of the same creative act, including the formation of woman, in Genesis 2:7, 21–23. See Gen. 2:4, *note* 5.

Man was created, not evolved. His body was formed by God from the dust of the earth; it did not develop from a protoplasm or germ cell. Man's soul did not come into being by chance, nor did it expand through processes of environment and selection. God breathed the breath of life into him and he became a living soul (Gen. 2:7).

Man's body and soul comprise a unity. Without the soul the body is dead. Without the body the soul is incomplete. When man's body dies the union is broken, but only temporarily; for the bodies of all who die will be raised, the righteous unto the resurrection of life and unbelieving sinners to the resurrection of judgment (Jn. 5:28–29; 1 Cor. 15:51–53; 1 Th. 4:14–17; Rev. 20:11–15).

A. The Material Part of Man

The material part of man is the active physical body which is visible. Formed of the dust of the ground, to the ground it will return (Gen. 2:7; 3:19).

Man's body may be thought of as that part of him which possesses sense consciousness. It is with his body that man sees, hears, and speaks. Tasting and smelling also are bodily functions. The body is sensitive to pain. In its voluntary operations the body is generally controlled by the soul working through the mind. There are certain essentials of life, however, in which the body's performances are not subject to the mind but operate automatically and even unconsciously, for example breathing, the beating of the heart, the flow of blood through the arteries, and digestive functioning. Yet so completely is the body merged with the soul that there is no sense of duality.* Man thinks of himself as residing within his body, as indeed he does. At the same time he considers his body to be himself, which indeed it is.

B. The Immaterial Part of Man

The immaterial part of man is that part which God breathed into him at his creation—the breath of life by which he was made a living soul. This God-breathed life is distinct from life in animals. It is the result of an act of God whereby the human body, differing from the body of every other creature, was made the recipient of a soul with an endless life. Because of sin the body dies. But the soul does not cease to exist at the death of the body, even though it is subject to death also. In addition to bodily death, there is that which is called the second death, which is the eternal state of the souls of all unregenerate sinners. See *notes* at Eph. 2:5; Rev. 20:14.

Man's soul can escape sin's penalty, the second death, by faith alone. When the sinner is reconciled to God through faith in the Lord Jesus Christ as his divine Substitute for sin, he receives another and different in-breathed life, a life imparted through

*In regard to man's tripartite nature, composed of body, soul, and spirit, see I Th. 5:23, *note*.

51

regeneration with the Holy Spirit (Ti. 3:5; cp. Jn. 20:22; Acts 2:1-4).

As the body of the first man, Adam, was the only human body formed by a direct creative act of God, so the soul of the first man was the only soul created by the life-giving breath of God. Ever since man's creation, the body and the soul have been inherited by natural generative process.

C. MAN'S ORIGINAL STATE

Three times in the Genesis accounts of man's creation it is stated that he was created in the image of God. This does not mean that in his corporeal form he is like God. "God is spirit" (Jn. 4:24). A spirit has neither flesh nor bones (cp. Lk. 24:39). So it was not in bodily appearance that man was created in the image and likeness of God.

In the New Testament regenerate men and women are instructed to "put on the new man, which after God is created in righteousness and holiness" (Eph. 4:23-24; cp. Col. 3:10). It may be inferred, therefore, that the image of God which was imparted to Adam was an image of righteousness, true holiness, and knowledge. Adam possessed intelligence, feelings, and will. See Gen. 1:26, *note* 1. He knew God and was in fellowship with Him. To him was given dominion over every living thing on earth, in the heavens, and in the waters. See Gen. 1:26, *note* 2. His intellect enabled him to name all God's creatures (Gen. 2:19-20). His mind was in tune with the mind of God. He was the possessor of righteousness and holiness, although these virtues may have been more passive than active inasmuch as he was created in innocence. However, Adam was without sin in his primal state and therefore righteous and holy in regard to the truth of God, until he was tempted by the devil and fell.

CHAPTER VII

Dispensations and Covenants

T HERE are a number of important turning points in Bible history. Some of them, but not all, bear a relationship to divine dispensations and covenants. Therefore these two terms are defined here so as to throw light on some of the historical crises referred to in chapters that follow.

1. Dispensations

Since the beginning of human history God has dealt with mankind in a progressive order. Over different time-periods man has been made responsible to Him under certain clearly defined circumstances. These distinctive time-periods are called dispensations, or economies, or stewardships. All students of the Bible are aware of the distinction between law and grace. Not all of them, however, recognize successive economies during which God has revealed Himself to mankind and in which man has been tested in specially appointed areas of response.

These tests of man's stewardship are not to be thought of as differing ways of redemption. Salvation has always been by God's grace through faith in the work of Christ in His death and resurrection, for even in Old Testament times salvation was prospective of Christ's atoning sacrifice. For example, under the dispensation of law the sinning Israelite brought an animal sacrifice to the tabernacle or temple to make a sin offering to God. See Lev. 4:3, *note*. The blood of the sacrificial bullock or lamb was shed, and the sacrifice served as a covering for the sinner's trespass (Heb. 10:4). The sinner's offering was an act of faith in God's promise of a Redeemer. See *notes* at Ex. 29:33; Lev. 16:6. In the economy of this present age, however, the sinning believer in Christ does not carry a lamb to an altar but confesses his sin to God, claiming the virtue of the blood of the sinless Christ, the Lamb of God, as the sacrifice which is wholly sufficient to satisfy God's holiness and justice (Heb. 9:11–15, 24–26; 10:12–18; 1 Pet. 1:18–21). In each instance the offering for sin is according to the divine demand in connection with a particular dispensation: the former under the Mosaic law and the latter in accordance with the dispensation of the Church. See *notes* at Ex. 19:1; Acts 2:1.

C. I. Scofield defined a dispensation as "a period of time during which man is tested in respect of obedience to some *specific* revelation of the will of God." Three things are implicit in this definition: (a) a revelation of what God requires of man, (b) man's stewardship of that revelation, and (c) a time-period during which such a test is in force. See *note* at Gen. 1:28, heading.

Although the dispensations are often referred to as ages (e.g. the age of Promise, the Church age, the Kingdom age), it should be kept in mind that frequently the deposit of truth concerning man's obedience to a divinely prescribed test during a specific time-period is not discarded as a stewardship, even though the dispensation itself may have been succeeded by a different economy. For example, although the age of Conscience (see Gen. 3:7 *note*) has terminated, conscience or moral responsibility continues as a stewardship of faith (e.g. Rom. 2:15; 9:1; 2 Cor. 1:12; 4:2).

Not all Bible students are in agreement concerning the number or names of the dispensations, but practically all concede the difference between the age of the Law and the Church age. Certainly a recognition of some distinction between God's dealings with man in different eras of Bible history is of highest value to an understanding of the Scriptures. In the NSRB seven dispensations are distinguished. They are designated as the Dispensation of Innocence (Gen. 1:28, *note* 1, p. 4), the Dispensation of Conscience or Moral Responsibility (Gen. 3:7, *note*), the Dispensation of Human Government (Gen. 8:15, *note*), the Dispensation of Promise (Gen. 12:1, *note* 1), the Dispensation of the Law (Ex. 19:1, *note*), the Church Dispensation (Acts 2:1, *note*), and the Dispensation of the Kingdom (Rev. 20:4, *note*).

2. *Covenants*

Linked closely with the dispensations are the covenants of God which bear upon man and his redemption. A divine covenant is a declaration by God concerning His voluntarily assumed responsibility in grace toward an individual, a family, a nation, or mankind as a whole. Generally God's covenants are unconditional. God declares that He will do such-and-such a thing to accomplish His purpose and does not abrogate that covenant whatever the human response may be. However, rewards for man's obedience and discipline for his disobedience will be given. See Gen. 2:16, *note* 1.

In the NSRB eight major covenants of significance in man's history are distinguished: the Edenic Covenant (Gen. 2:16-19; see v. 16, *note* 2), the Adamic Covenant (Gen. 3:14-19; see v. 15, *note* 2), the Noachin Covenant (Gen. 9:8-17; see v. 16, *note*), the Abrahamic Covenant (Gen. 12:1-3; 13:14-17; 15:1-5, 18-21; 17:1-8; see Gen. 12:2, *note*), the Mosaic Covenant (Ex. 19:3-6; see v. 5, *note* 2), the Palestinian Covenant (Dt. 30:1-10; see v. 3, *note*), the Davidic Covenant (2 Sam. 7:4-17; see v. 16, *note*), and the New Covenant (Heb. 8:7-12; see v. 8, *notes* 1 and 2).

The Edenic Covenant was made with Adam and required certain responsibilities on his part relating to the Garden of Eden. The Adamic Covenant (spoken to the serpent, to Eve, and to Adam) and the Noachin Covenant (made with Noah) are universal. The next four covenants—the Abrahamic (given to Abraham), the Mosaic and Palestinian (made with Israel through Moses), and the Davidic (given to David through Nathan)—apply to Israel primarily, with ultimate blessing promised for the whole world. The New Covenant is made with all believers in Christ, whether Jews or Gentiles.

The individual dispensations and covenants are discussed more fully in their proper settings.

CHAPTER VIII

Some Important Turning Points
in Biblical History: Old Testament

IN the course of God's dealings with mankind there have been
and are yet to be great turning points which are rooted in
biblical history and prophecy. It is not by chance but under the
sovereign will of God that events occur that alter human history.
The crises of the Old Testament and the circumstances surrounding them are the subject of this chapter.

Keep in mind, in thinking about man's history, that the men
and women of the past ages were, as James said of Elijah, "subject
to like passions as we are" (Jas. 5:17). The temptations and trials
they knew are also ours today; the failures they experienced may
also be ours. Yet in this present age we have a fuller revelation of
divine grace than they had, and believers in Christ have the inestimable advantage of the indwelling Spirit of God.

1. *The Fall of Man*

The first man, Adam, was created in the image and likeness
of God. See Gen. 1:26, *note*. God made a covenant with Adam.
He placed him in a perfect environment and gave him dominion
over every living thing. Adam's responsibility was to cultivate
the garden and to obey God. Created as he was, without knowing
by personal experience the difference between good and evil, Adam
was subjected by God to a single test—"of the tree of the knowledge of good and evil thou shalt not eat"—and warned of the
consequence of disobedience—"for in the day that thou eatest
thereof thou shalt surely die" (Gen. 2:17, where see *note*). See
also Edenic Covenant, Gen. 2:16, *notes* 1 and 2. Man failed under

this stewardship. Eve was tempted by Satan in the guise of a serpent, and yielded to the devil's craftiness. She and Adam ate of the fruit of the tree. They were expelled from Eden (Gen. 3—4). So ended the first dispensation. See Dispensation of Innocence, Gen. 1:28, *note*.

This was the first turning point recorded in biblical history. For with his fall into sin through rebellion against God, man became a sinner and was separated from his Creator. By his fall he brought sin upon the whole race, and death also.

2. *The Flood*

At the expulsion of Adam and Eve from Eden, God made another covenant with Adam (Gen. 3:14-17). See Adamic Covenant, Gen. 3:15, *note*. Included among its elements were the first promise of a Redeemer (Gen. 3:15), the necessity of labor on man's part (vv. 18-19), and the certainty of physical death (v. 19; cp. Rom. 5:12-21). Having entered the realm of moral experience through sin, man was placed by God under the stewardship of conscience or moral responsibility and made accountable to do all known good and to abstain from all known evil. His approach to God was not direct, as it had been in the Garden of Eden, but through the intermediary offering of a blood sacrifice (e.g. Gen. 4:4, where see *note*), which was symbolic of the blood of Christ that would be shed at Calvary (1 Pet. 1:18-21; cp. Heb. 9:22).

Again man failed. Cain, the first male born on earth, murdered his brother Abel. Cain had brought an offering to God that was not in accord with the divine will and was rejected (Gen. 4:3, 5), whereas Abel's blood sacrifice was accepted by God (v. 4; cp. Heb. 11:4). In a fit of rage Cain killed his brother (v. 8).

Time passed and sin began to pervade all of man's life, so that "every imagination of the thoughts of his heart was only evil continually" (Gen. 6:5). As a result divine judgment in the flood fell upon the whole race excepting Noah and his family (Gen. 7:1—8:14).

This was the second turning point for mankind in biblical history. The Dispensation of Conscience or Moral Responsibility ended and man was placed under another economy. However, whereas moral responsibility ceased as the specific test in relation to man's obedience to God, conscience continues as a stewardship of faith even to the present time (e.g. Rom. 2:15; 2 Cor. 4:2). See Dispensation of Conscience, Gen. 3:7, *note*.

3. *The Confusion of Tongues*

The deluge had ceased, the flood waters had abated. Noah disembarked from the ark with his family and the creatures that were with them during the flood, built an altar, and offered a sacrifice to God (Gen. 8:21—9:17). God reaffirmed to Noah what He had covenanted with Adam concerning conditions of life on earth, but among the additional elements in the covenant with Noah were the promise that there would be no further curse upon the earth (8:21; cp. 3:17–19), the seasons of the year and their harvests would not fail (8:22), and the flesh of animals would now be added to man's diet (9:3–4—evidently prior to this time men had been vegetarians). The covenant affirmed the sanctity of human life (9:6), and God promised that never again would there be a flood that would destroy men and beasts (9:11, 15). The rainbow was revealed as the designated token of God's covenant between Himself and every living creature on the earth (9:16–17). See Noachin Covenant, Gen. 9:16; *note*.

Man was subjected to a new test of stewardship. His direct moral responsibility to God was not abrogated, but in the new dispensation he was made accountable to Him for his submissiveness to his fellow men. In this corporate relationship between men, governmental authority was invested with the right of capital punishment as a safeguard of the sanctity of human life. Not individual vengeance but only civil requital was thus licensed. The economy under which Noah began his postdiluvian life on earth is known as the Dispensation of Human Government. See Gen. 8:15, *note*.

Again man failed. This failure was demonstrated in the building of a city and the tower of Babel, whose top was to reach to heaven (Gen. 11:1–4). Here was a consolidated attempt on man's part to make a name for himself. It is notable that the name of God is omitted from the express purpose of the quest: "Come, let *us* make brick . . . let *us* build *us* a city and a tower . . . let *us* make *us* a name." Perhaps they wanted to worship the stars rather than God. Certainly Babel was man's first effort to establish a one-world government in opposition to divine rule (v. 6), a dramatic prototype of the essence of man's rebellion against God, of his desire to "go it alone" apart from God. This is a pattern repeated throughout history down to our time (e.g. Ps. 2:1ff.). So the Lord acted in judgment by confounding the language (vv. 5–9), for previously "the whole earth was of one language and of one speech" (v. 1). Man had failed to govern himself righteously. See Rom. 1:18–32, with *note* at v. 18.

This was the third turning point in biblical history. As a result of the Babel incident men were scattered abroad and God turned to one man, then to his family, and finally to the nation that developed out of this family, in order to bring His blessing to the whole world.

4. *The Call of Abram*

From the creation of Adam until man's failure at Babel, although there had come into being certain national distinctions (see Gen. 10:1, *note*), there were no Jews. Abram was of the nations, what we today would call a Gentile. The call of Abram (later known as Abraham, Gen. 17:5, and so called hereafter in this book) was the fourth major turning point in God's dealings with mankind. The record begins in Genesis 11:10. As the result of Abraham's call, a nation, Israel, was separated from the mainstream of humanity to be a witness concerning the divine unity, to illustrate the blessedness of serving God, to receive and guard the divine revelations to men, and to be the human channel for the coming of the Messiah, the Lord Jesus Christ. See Gen. 11:10, *note* 7, p. 17.

Somewhere in the early part of the twentieth century B.C. Abraham left Ur in Chaldea with Sarai his wife (later known as Sarah, Gen. 17:15), Terah his father, and his nephew Lot and his wife to go to the land of Canaan. But upon coming to Haran they remained there until the death of Terah. Before this, while Abraham was still in Ur, the Lord had said to him, "Get thee out of thy country, and from thy kindred, and from thy father's house, unto a land that I will show thee; and I will make of thee a great nation, and I will bless thee, and make thy name great; and thou shalt be a blessing. And I will bless them that bless thee, and curse him that curseth thee: and in thee shall all families of the earth be blessed" (Gen. 12:1–3).

This covenant that God made with Abraham was confirmed and enlarged on later occasions (Gen. 13:14–17; 15:1–7, 18–21; 17:1–8; 22:15–18; 26:1–5; 28:13–15; 35:9–12). It involved personal promises to Abraham both temporal and spiritual. Temporally, not only would Abraham's name be great but he would also acquire land, cattle, beasts of burden, servants, and monetary wealth as well as descendants as numerous "as the dust of the earth" (Gen. 13:16; 17:16). To him and his descendants God gave everlasting possession of Canaan. Spiritually, God covenanted to bless Abraham and count his faith for righteousness and to be his God (Gen. 12:2; 15:6; 17:7–8; cp. Rom. 4:3; Gal. 3:6), in addition to the promise already mentioned, that Abraham and his descendants would be the channel for the coming of the Messiah.

Abraham would be the father of the nation Israel and also the "father" of those Gentiles who would believe God as Abraham did; for in him would "all the families of the earth be blessed" (Gen. 12:3). This promise was to find its fulfillment in Christ (Gal. 3:6–9, 29). See Abrahamic Covenant, Gen. 12:2, *note*.

The stewardship of faith under which Abraham was placed required his obedience (Gen. 22:18; 26:5). As a dispensation, it extended from Abraham's call to the giving of the Mosaic law.

However, the covenant with Abraham and his seed was not abrogated at Sinai. References concerning Israel's everlasting inheritance of Canaan appear in the later portions of the O.T. and in the N.T. as well (Gal. 3:17–18; cp. Ex. 32:13; Lev. 25:2; Dt. 6:1; Josh. 1:2; Rom. 9:4). See Dispensation of Promise, Gen. 12:1, *note* 1.

Temporal blessing under Abraham's stewardship of faith was associated with his remaining in the land of promise. Now Abraham is notable in biblical history as a man of faith. Paul called him "faithful Abraham" (Gal. 3:9). His obedience and the greatness of his faith were demonstrated in his readiness to offer his son Isaac as a sacrifice when God commanded him to do so (Gen. 22:1–14). Yet, like other men, Abraham was not perfect. When famine came upon the land, he departed from Bethel and went down into Egypt. The result was a lapse into sin (Gen. 12:10–20). Only when he realized his mistake and returned to Bethel, where he built an altar and confessed his transgression to God, was he again in the place of blessing.

Years later another famine came to Canaan. Abraham's grandson Jacob (also called Israel, Gen. 32:28) left the land of Canaan with his family and went to Egypt so that they might be sustained through the favor of Joseph, who was already there in a position of authority. It is significant that after Jacob had begun his journey, God spoke to him in a night vision, saying, "Fear not to go down into Egypt; for I will there make of thee a great nation: I will go down with thee into Egypt; and I will surely bring thee up again" (Gen. 46:3–4). Even though God predicted what would happen, Jacob's journey to Egypt may possibly have been under His permissive will rather than His directive will. Whatever the circumstance, Jacob's act of expediency led to Israel's enslavement in Egypt for a period of four centuries.

5. *The Emigration to Egypt*

When Jacob, with his sons and their children, entered Egypt he was given a place of privilege. This was because of the favor that Joseph, his son, had found with Pharaoh, who said to Joseph, "Thy father and thy brethren have come unto thee. The land of Egypt is before thee; in the best of the land make thy father and thy brethren to dwell; in the land of Goshen let them dwell" (Gen. 47:5–6).

However, with the passing of the years the seventy children of Israel multiplied greatly, so much so that after a little more than three centuries there were a million or more of them in Egypt. Another Pharaoh now sat on the throne. He had not known Joseph, of course, and Joseph's name meant little or nothing to him. The Hittites were threatening to invade Egypt. Pharaoh feared that, should war come, the Israelites might unite with the enemy against him. So Egypt's ruler enslaved God's chosen people and compelled them to build cities and storehouses out of bricks that they themselves were obliged to make, and to work in the fields to produce food for Egypt's wartime needs. This was a time of frustration and affliction for the children of Israel. But the more they were maltreated, the more they multiplied. All this is told in Exodus 1.

This was the fifth turning point in biblical history—not the emigration of the Israelites from Canaan to a foreign land, but the fact that they remained there. From Abraham's call until the time Jacob went down to Egypt, Abraham's descendants comprised a family of about seventy people. It was in Egypt that they began to have a national history. God had not forsaken them. His promises were still valid. Joseph's brothers had acted wickedly in selling him to a party of Midianites and Ishmaelites (Gen. 37). Jacob's faith had weakened so that he and his family settled in Egypt. Yet God brought good out of evil. As Joseph told his brothers, "Ye thought evil against me, but God meant it for good" (Gen. 50:20). His betrayal by his brothers resulted in due time in blessing upon the whole family. Out of the suffering of God's people in Egypt in later years, God demonstrated His love and mercy and power in redeeming them by His own hand when the proper time came. He raised up a deliverer for Israel to bring them back to the place of blessing. So centuries later, God the Father was to give His beloved Son to deliver us from the bondage of sin into the place of blessedness with Himself.

6. *The Exodus*

The record of Moses' birth and preservation in Egypt and God's preparation of him appears in Exodus 3—11.

In reading of the contest of wills between God's servant and Egypt's king it should be remembered that, as with all the characters of biblical history, real people were involved. Pharaoh was perhaps the world's most powerful ruler at that time. Moses, a Hebrew, was the adopted son of Pharaoh's daughter (Ex. 2:1–10) and was therefore accustomed to the splendor of the palace and to dealing with royalty. He had also known solitude as a shepherd in the land of Midian (Ex. 2:11–22; see Ex. 16:35, *note* 2). Moses was a man of meekness (Num. 12:3), which suggests that his character and strength were like Christ's (Mt. 11:29; 2 Cor. 10:1; cp. Mt. 5:5). In many ways Moses' life and work are typical of the earthly life and ministry of Jesus Christ. See Ex. 2:2, *note*. In the N.T. it is said that Moses chose "rather to suffer affliction with the people of God than to enjoy the pleasures of sin for a season, esteeming the reproach of Christ greater riches than the treasures in Egypt; for he had respect unto the recompense of the reward" (Heb. 11:24-26).

The angel of the Lord (i.e. the Son Himself, see Jud. 2:1, *note*) met with Moses at Mt. Horeb in the desert of Midian and spoke to him from the burning bush. There God told Moses that he was to be the deliverer of the children of Israel (Ex. 3:1—4:17). Moses returned to Egypt and told Pharaoh, "Thus saith the LORD God of Israel, Let my people go" (Ex. 5:1). This was the first of ten meetings that Moses had with Egypt's ruler. Each time the king's heart was hardened and he rejected Moses' plea even though on many of these occasions frightful plagues fell upon the land. See Ex. 7:20, *note*. At length God's patience with Pharaoh ended and He hardened Pharaoh's heart again. See Ex. 4:21, *note*.

Now He brought to pass an event which was a great turning point in the history of Israel.

First, the Lord instituted the Passover Feast. See Ex. 12:11, *note*. Every household of Israel was to take a lamb and, at the appointed time, kill the lamb and sprinkle its blood on the two doorposts and over the door of the house. That same night they were to eat the lamb, roasted and served with bitter herbs and unleavened bread. The people were to be dressed for a journey, for this was to be the night of their deliverance from slavery in Egypt (Ex. 12:1–11).

At midnight the Lord would pass through Egypt. All the first-born males in Egypt would be slain that night, Egyptians and Israelites, except in those houses where the blood of a lamb was on the doorposts. For God had said to Moses, "When I see the blood, I will pass over you, and the plague shall not be upon you to destroy you, when I smite the land of Egypt" (Ex. 12:13). The Lord did so, and that night His people began their departure from Egypt, "from Rameses to Succoth, about six hundred thousand on foot that were men, beside children" (v. 37). This event probably took place about 1447 B.C.*

In the Passover lamb the perceptive reader of the Bible must surely discern a figure of Christ and His sacrifice. He is the true Lamb of God (Jn. 1:29, 36), the ultimate deliverer of His people (1 Pet. 1:18–21). Indeed, He is designated in the N.T. as "Christ, our passover" (1 Cor. 5:7).

The O.T. should be read with Christ in view, for He is shown there in type and symbol again and again (1 Cor. 10:11). He told the Jews of His time to "search the Scriptures, for . . . they are they which testify of me" (Jn. 5:39). And after His resurrection Christ pointed out to the two disciples on the way to Emmaus that they should have known of His death and the glory that would follow, "and beginning at Moses and all the prophets, he expounded unto them in all the scriptures the things concerning himself" (Lk. 24:25–27).

*Some scholars date the event in the thirteenth century B.C. But the editors of the NSRB felt that evidence favors the earlier date.

More than four centuries after Jacob left the land of promise, the Israelites were on their way back. The journey was to take forty years.

God's care of His people was constantly demonstrated in their wilderness experience. To guide them the Lord went before them by day in a pillar of cloud and by night in a pillar of fire. When Pharaoh pursued them the Lord opened the waters of the Red Sea to allow them to pass to the other side and then closed the sea upon their pursuers. He provided food and drink in a miraculous way—sweet water from bitter water, manna from heaven, and water from a rock to sustain them in a barren land. All these things are recorded in Exodus 12—18. See *notes* at Ex. 15:25; 16:35, *note* 1; 17:6.

Israel, once an enslaved people in the land of Egypt, became a nomad nation on the way to a land of plenty. They came to the Sinai desert about three months after their escape from Pharaoh (Ex. 19:1-2). There something of major significance occurred.

7. *The Law of Moses*

To Abraham, Isaac, and Jacob, God had made an unchangeable promise concerning their inheritance of Canaan and had covenanted that through Abraham's descendants blessing should come upon the whole world. It was expected of the Israelites that they would obey God's voice. However, as man had failed under earlier stewardships, he failed again in his responsibility of faith and obedience.

When the children of Israel pitched their camp at Mt. Sinai they must have numbered well over a million men, women, and children. They needed clarification of their relationship with God and their fellow men. In order to institute an orderly system of behavior on their part, God met with Moses and instructed him to tell the people, "Ye have seen what I did unto the Egyptians, and how I bore you on eagles' wings and brought you unto myself. Now therefore, if you will obey my voice indeed, and keep my covenant, then ye shall be a peculiar treasure unto me above all

65

people; for all the earth is mine: and ye shall be unto me a king-dom of priests, and an holy nation" (Ex. 19:4–6). Thereupon a new economy was introduced and a new covenant formed. God gave them the law. See Dispensation of the Law, Ex. 19:1, *note*; Mosaic Covenant, Ex. 19:5, *note* 2. This was the seventh turning point in biblical history.

The Mosaic law consists of more than the Decalogue or Ten Commandments, although the Decalogue may be said to epitomize the law. The law of Moses is in three parts: (a) the Ten Command-ments, which expressed God's righteous will for His people (Ex. 20:1–17); (b) the judgments, which dealt with the relation-ships of the Israelites with one another (Ex. 21:1—24:8); and (c) the ordinances, which governed Israel's religious life (Ex. 25:1—31:19). Introductory to each of the three parts is a demonstration of the awesome holiness of God (Ex. 19:9–25; 20:18–26; 24:9–18).

The law did not abrogate the Abrahamic Covenant (Gen. 12:1–2; Gal. 3:17–18) nor did it offer redemption or justification before God. It was a way *of* life for a people already in covenant relationship with God, not a way *to* life (Gal. 2:15–16; 3:21). It presented a perfect standard to show men they are sinners. With this righteous standard, God graciously provided blood sacrifices to cover the sins of the people for the time being and to enable them to enter His holy Presence. The sacrifices under the law were symbols or types (see Gen. 2:23, *notes*; cp. Ex. 25:1, *note*) of the vicarious, atoning death of the Lord Jesus Christ. The law was the guardian of God's people and, as their "schoolmaster," taught them by means of prophetic sacrifices until Christ came and offered Himself as the perfect Sacrifice for sin. See *notes* at Gal. 3:24, 25.

To see in the exodus from Egypt a historical event only, without perceiving that the Passover lamb was typical of Christ, the Lamb of God, is a mistake. Likewise the ordinances of the law should not be read without taking into account that repeatedly Christ was foreshadowed in the religious life of the Israelites; for instance, in many of the materials that went into the building of the tabernacle, as well as in its furnishings and offerings (Ex. 25:31). See *notes* at Ex. 25:9, 10, 30, 31; 26:1, 15, 19, 31; etc.).

Two things should be clearly understood about the Mosaic law. (a) It did not provide a means of salvation. This cannot be emphasized too strongly. The law condemns; it does not give life (2 Cor. 3:7, 9). God gave it to show men they are sinners and to point to the divine provision of sacrifice for sin. And (b) God's grace was equally as efficient under the economy of the law as it is in the present age. Salvation has been, is, and always will be by divine grace through faith in God and not by works of righteousness on man's part (Eph. 2:8–9; Ti. 3:4–7).

As time went on some of the Israelites began to misinterpret the purpose of the law, supposing that by their own good deeds and observance of ritualistic ordinances they could be redeemed (Rom. 9:31—10:9; cp. Acts 15:1). "The law is holy, and the commandment holy, and just, and good" (Rom. 7:12), but man is a sinner and in his unregenerate state cannot keep it. However, "what the law could not do, in that it was weak through the flesh, God sending His own Son in the likeness of sinful flesh and for sin, condemned sin in the flesh, that the righteousness of the law might be fulfilled in us [believers in Christ as Lord and Saviour], who walk not after the flesh but after the Spirit" (Rom. 8:3–4).

As a stewardship of faith the Mosaic law continued until the formation of the Church. Under the law Israel failed—in the wilderness journey, in Canaan under the prophets and kings, and in their dispersion in later years— as man has always failed. For after they received the law at the hand of Moses, with God graciously guiding them by the pillars of fire and cloud, feeding them in the desert, showing them His Presence in the tabernacle, and offering a covering for their sins by animal sacrifices, they went their way until they were within sight of the land of promise. Then, in unbelief, they rebelled against God.

8. *Kadesh-barnea*

Approximately two years after the Israelites departed from Egypt they reached Kadesh-barnea, a short distance south of the promised land. The Lord told Moses to send twelve men, each a leader of one of the tribes of Israel, to discover what they could about Canaan (Num. 13). So Moses sent them out. The men came back after forty days with grapes, pomegranates, and figs and reported their findings to Moses and the people.

The twelve men who searched Canaan seem to have been in agreement about its productivity, saying that "surely it floweth with milk and honey, and this [the grapes, pomegranates, and figs] is the fruit of it." A majority report was made by ten frightened men who complained that the Israelites could not possibly go up against the giants who inhabited Canaan. But in a minority report Caleb and Joshua, having faith in the promise and power of God, urged the people, "Let us go up at once, and possess it; for we are well able to overcome it."

Numbers 14 describes a rebellious nation and God's disciplinary dealings with them. The Israelites wept in great fear after hearing of the alleged giant stature of the men of Canaan, and cried out to Moses, "Would God that we had died in the land of Egypt! Or would God we had died in this wilderness!" (v. 2). Some of them suggested that a new leader be chosen to take Moses' place and that they should return to Egypt. They actually wanted to stone Caleb and Joshua. So the Lord was ready to send pestilence on them, disinherit them because of unbelief, and even appoint another nation composed of Moses' descendants as His witness on earth. But in response to Moses' plea, the Lord pardoned faithless Israel whom He still loved. However, He had to punish them severely (cp. Heb. 12:6).

Since they had left Egypt, Israel had provoked the Lord no less than ten times (Num. 14:22). See (1) Ex. 14:11–12; (2) 15:23–24; (3) 16:2–3; (4) 16:19–20; (5) 16:27–28; (6) 17:1–4; (7) 32:7–10; (8) Num. 11:1; (9) 11:4–6; (10) 13:31—14:5. It was on this last occasion that they expressed the wish that they might have died in Egypt or in the wilderness. "All right," the Lord said in effect, "that is precisely what will happen to you. Every one of you from twenty years of age and up, excepting Caleb and Joshua, will die in the wilderness. Only your children will enter the land you have despised and refused to enter. When they get there at last, they will have wandered in the wilderness for forty years, one year for every day that your leaders searched out Canaan" (see Num. 14:20–38).

When they heard this, the Israelites turned around and decided to go immediately into the land of promise. Acting in unbelief, they tried to enter Canaan but were routed by the Amalekites and Canaanites (vv. 39–45).

A journey that ought to have been completed in two years took forty years because a redeemed people who had seen God working in power on their behalf disregarded His promise and rebelled against Him. See *notes* at Num. 14:23; 15:1. The N.T. uses the wilderness experiences of the children of Israel and this eighth turning point in biblical history as the source of many lessons for and admonitions to believers of this present age (1 Cor. 10:1–11; Heb. 3:16–19).

9. *The Conquest of Canaan*

The opening sentence of the book of Joshua contains the Lord's command to Joshua, "Moses, my servant, is dead; now therefore arise, go over this Jordan, thou and all this people, unto the land which I do give them, even to the children of Israel" (Josh. 1:1–2). This statement, which is an essential prologue to the record of the conquest of Canaan, requires of the reader a backward and a forward look.

"Moses, my servant, is dead." The continuity of God's program cannot be interrupted by the death of one of His servants, no matter how valuable that man or woman may have been to Him. Moses was dead but the divine promise would be fulfilled. But why did not Moses lead them into the land of promise and take possession of it, an event for which they had waited so long? The book of Numbers gives the answer.

At Meribah the long-suffering Moses became provoked with Israel. Because there was no water and the Israelites were thirsty, they reverted to their old complaint, "Would God we had died! Why have you made us come up out of Egypt?" The Lord told Moses to take his rod and to speak to the rock before the eyes of the people, saying that water would come out of the rock (cp. I Cor. 10:4; see Ex. 17:6, *note*). But Moses' patience was exhausted. Angrily he called the people rebels, asking them, "Must we fetch you water out of this rock?" (as though it were by his and Aaron's power rather than God's that the water would be supplied). Then, in a rage, Moses struck the rock twice with the rod instead of speaking to it as he was commanded. As a consequence the Lord said to him, "Because ye believed me not, to sanctify me in the eyes of the children of Israel, therefore ye shall not bring this congregation into the land which I have given them" (see Num. 20:1–13; Dt. 1:37; 31:2).

Shortly before his death Moses spoke to the congregation about the conditions they would face when they should go into the promised land. At the same time God made a covenant with Israel. "These are the words of the covenant which the LORD commanded Moses to make with the children of Israel in the land of Moab, beside the covenant that he made with them at Horeb" (Dt. 29:1).

Forty years had passed since the covenant was made at Horeb (Mt. Sinai), a covenant embodying the Mosaic law. See Mosaic Covenant, Ex. 19:5, *note* 2. The covenant of Moab did not abrogate the Sinai Covenant but supplemented it. This Palestinian Covenant states that Israel's obedience after they enter the land will bring blessing (Dt. 29:9–15), warns that disobedience will result in dispersion (29:16–29), declares that their restoration and the judgment of their oppressors will depend upon repentance on Israel's part (30:1–10), and commands them to love the Lord and keep His commandments so that they may dwell in the land which He swore unto their fathers to give them (30:11–20). See Palestinian Covenant, Dt. 30:3, *note*.

"So Moses, the servant of the LORD, died there in the land of Moab, according to the word of the LORD." Because of divine discipline, Moses never entered Canaan, but through divine grace he was permitted to see the land from Mt. Pisgah in the company of the Lord (Dt. 34:1–5).

So, then, after the death of Moses, God said to Joshua, "Go over this Jordan, thou and all this people, unto the land which I do give to them, even to the children of Israel" (Josh. 1:2). Joshua was a man who possessed both faith and courage. It will be recalled how he and Caleb brought in a minority report when the twelve spies had searched out Canaan thirty-eight years earlier at Kadesh-barnea (Num. 14:6–9). Joshua's close association with Moses and his military experience in the war with the Amalakites qualified him for the leadership of Israel (Ex. 17:8–16). Above all he was God's choice as Moses' successor (Num. 27:18–23; Dt. 1:38), and when God gave him his commission He promised to be with him wherever he should go (Josh. 1:3–9).

As Joshua was making preparation to cross the Jordan River into Canaan he sent two spies to view the land, especially Jericho, where the initial confrontation was to take place (Josh. 1:10—2:24). The Israelites were entering upon what was clearly a holy enterprise (e.g. Josh. 3:3, 5; 5:10). The Lord opened the waters of the Jordan River for the children of Israel as previously He had divided the Red Sea. So He proved He was with Joshua as He had been with Moses forty years before (cp. Ex. 14:13–31). The Israelites, preceded by their priests bearing the ark of the covenant (see Ex. 25:10. *note*), crossed dry-shod into Canaan (Josh. 3—4). Before they engaged in a single battle a man appeared to Joshua near Jericho and introduced himself as "captain of the host of the LORD" for the conflict that would follow (5:13–16). This "man" was doubtless the preincarnate Son of God. See Gen. 12:7, *note* 1.

The Israelites would conquer Canaan and dwell there, but not without occasional defeat. Their victories were won with supernatural help. Their defeats came upon them because of disobedience. A notable example of their triumphs was the conquest of Jericho. After Israel's warriors and priests, the latter carrying the ark of the covenant, had marched around the city once each day for six days and seven times on the seventh day, the priests blew their trumpets as God had commanded. The walls of the city tumbled down (Josh. 6:1–21). Conspicuous among their defeats was the humiliating loss at Ai which came as a result of the sin of one man, Achan (ch. 7). Later, when the sin had been confessed and judgment executed upon the offender, the siege of Ai was successful (ch. 8).

Actually the conquest of Canaan was not fully accomplished under Joshua. Israel never took possession of the whole land. However, Joshua's chronicle ends with the children of Israel living as a nation in the land Jacob and his immediate family had left so many years before.

10. *The Kingdom*

The kingdom of God on earth is a vast subject. It is a phase of the universal kingdom of God which has always existed and which embraces all objects and events, including the actions of nations and individuals (Ps. 103:19; cp. Dan. 4:17, where see *note*). The earthly aspect of the theocratic kingdom began when God entrusted Adam with sovereignty over creation. See Gen. 1:26, *note*. Because of sin, man lost dominion over the earth and Satan became the "prince of this world" (Jn. 14:30; cp. Mt. 4:8–10). But God re-established human government on earth following the flood, when He made a covenant with Noah, even though Satan was permitted to retain his place as the "prince of the power of the air" (Eph. 2:2), the unseen ruler of the world system. See Noachin Covenant, Gen. 9:16, *note* 2. Specifically, it is the kingdom of God in relation to Israel that finds its place among the turning points of the Bible.*

A. The Kingdom of Israel

After the Israelites' entrance into the land of promise, the nation was governed by divinely appointed leaders, such as Joshua and the judges. There were thirteen judges in all (twelve men and one woman), whose rule was generally successive, though some- times concurrent like that of Deborah and Barak (Jud. 4—5), until

*For discussion of the kingdom of heaven and the millennial kingdom see Ch. X, p. 93ff., Ch. XV, p. 151.

the days of Samuel the prophet. Samuel was also a priest and at the same time the last of the judges. Near the end of his life the people demanded that he appoint a king like other nations had, to rule over them (1 Sam. 8:5). This displeased the Lord. However, He acceded to their request, warning them of the consequences (vv. 6–22). See 1 Sam. 8:7, *note*. So God chose Saul to be Israel's first king. The record of Saul's failures and death, and the anointing and accession of David to the throne, are recorded in 1 Samuel 10—2 Samuel 5.

The reign of King Saul was actually a bridge between the period of the judges and King David. For it was to David and his seed that God covenanted an everlasting kingdom on the earth (Ps. 89:3–4), the ultimate promise pointing to David's greater Son, the Lord Jesus Christ. God promised David that He would give him perpetual posterity, a throne, and a kingdom that would be established forever (2 Sam. 7:8–17). See Davidic Covenant, 2 Sam. 7:16, *note*. Under David, Israel destroyed some of their enemies, drove others out of the land, and subdued still others, who were allowed to remain in Palestine. David also quelled rebellions within the nation (e.g. Absalom's, 2 Sam. 15:1—18:20, and Sheba's, 2 Sam. 20). He made restitution to the Gibeonites, who had been wronged. The record of David's reign is given in 2 Samuel 6—24 and also in portions of 1 Chronicles.*

At David's death his son Solomon became the king of Israel. David had wanted to build a house for the Lord, a permanent temple. It was not God's will that David should do this, because David was a man of war (1 Chr. 22:6–10). So the Lord told David, "Thou shalt not build me an house to dwell in; for I have not dwelt in an house since the day that I brought up Israel unto this day, but have gone from tent to tent, and from one tabernacle to another." See 2 Sam. 7:1–17; 1 Chr. 17:1–15.

Solomon's reign began on a very high plane. As his initial act he offered a sacrifice to God and prayed in great humility for an understanding heart and divine wisdom to rule justly. God

---

*It is significant that beginning with David no one ever sat or will sit upon David's throne except his descendants, including Jesus Christ, who was in the royal line (Mt. 1:1; Lk. 3:31; Rom. 1:3; Rev. 22:16).

answered this prayer (1 Ki. 3:3–14; 2 Chr. 1:1–12). Solomon began building the temple and completed it in seven years. He dedicated it with a remarkably beautiful prayer (1 Ki. 8:22–53; 2 Chr. 6:12–42). Solomon's wealth and fame increased. His reputation reached far and wide—to Egypt and Sheba (possibly Ethiopia), and among the Ammonites, Edomites, Sidonians, and Hittites. But his riches and many foreign wives led him away from God. After a reign of forty years he died a chastened man, knowing that his kingdom would be divided (1 Ki. 3—11; 2 Chr. 2—9).

B. The Kingdom Divided

Rehoboam, Solomon's son, was anointed king at Shechem. While he was there Jeroboam, the son of Nebat, one of Solomon's servants, came to him and pled with him to ease the heavy burden of servitude Solomon had imposed on the people. Rehoboam consulted the older men. They advised him to heed Jeroboam's entreaty. But younger men urged Rehoboam to say, "Whereas my father put a heavy yoke upon you, I will put more to your yoke; my father chastened you with whips, but I will chastise you with scorpions." Rehoboam accepted this advice. When the people heard this, all the tribes of Israel except Judah and Benjamin turned away from Rehoboam and made Jeroboam their king. The kingdom thus was divided (1 Ki. 12; 2 Chr. 10). King Rehoboam reigned over the two loyalist tribes, Judah and Benjamin, which together became known as Judah or the southern kingdom. Jeroboam ruled the other ten tribes, still called Israel in distinction from Judah, and known also as the northern kingdom. See 2 Chr. 10:16, *note*. Other names for the ten tribes are Ephraim and Samaria (2 Chr. 25:7; cp. 2 Ki. 17:6). See Isa. 7:2, *note*.

In reading the books of Kings and Chronicles the identity of the kings and their kingdoms is sometimes puzzling. Keep in mind, therefore, these two things:

(1) So as to preserve the record of the reign of each king without interruption, whether of Judah or Israel, these books register each reign from beginning to end even though, during certain reigns, one or more kings may have been enthroned in the other kingdom. For example, Asa reigned over Judah for forty-one

years, *c.* 911–870 B.C. (1 Ki. 15:9–24). During that same period five kings of Israel began and concluded their reigns: Nadab (1 Ki. 15:25–31), Baasha (15:32—16:7), Elah (16:8–10), Zimri (16:10–20), and Omri (16:23–27). Their combined reigns covered about thirty-six years, *c.* 910–874 B.C., after which Ahab began his twenty-two-year rule over Israel *c.* 874–853. Asa was still king of Judah, however. He died in 870 B.C. And although Jehoshaphat succeeded him immediately (1 Ki. 15:24), the record of Jehoshaphat's reign over Judah does not interrupt the history of Ahab of Israel. Only after Ahab's death in 853 B.C., which was seventeen years after Jehoshaphat ascended the throne of Judah, is an account of Jehoshaphat's reign given. Then it is recorded, "And Jehoshaphat, the son of Asa, began to reign over Judah in the fourth year of Ahab, king of Israel" (1 Ki. 22:41).

(2) A set form is followed in introducing the reigns of the kings of Israel and Judah. This form is much the same for the kings of both nations, except that in the case of the kings of Judah two additional facts are given—the age of the king at the beginning of his reign and the name of his mother. Compare 2 Kings 8:25–26 with 2 Kings 13:1

Saul, David, and Solomon ruled a united Israel from 1050 to 931 B.C., at which time the kingdom was divided (1 Sam. 9—31; 1 Chr. 11—2 Chr. 9). The northern kingdom, Israel, which began in 931 B.C., continued until the Assyrian captivity in about 721 B.C. The southern kingdom, Judah, lasted 135 years longer (1 Ki. 2:1—2 Ki. 25:30; 2 Chr. 10:1—36:21). Then Jerusalem fell and its inhabitants were taken captive by Babylon in 586 B.C.

Some of the kings of Judah were good; some were evil. No king of Israel was good. Like all men, the good kings of Judah sinned at times. A few of the wicked kings accomplished some meritorious things. The over-all picture is a bad one. God, who looks at men's hearts rather than at their outward appearance (1 Sam. 16:7), gives through the writers of the books of Samuel, Kings, and Chronicles His estimate of all the kings of Israel and Judah, characterizing them as those who did right or evil in His sight. There follows a tabulation of the kings of the northern and southern kingdoms. See also 1 Ki. 12:19, *note.*

75

KINGS OF ISRAEL AND JUDAH

Israel	Reign	God's Estimate
Jeroboam I	931–910 B.C.	Evil
Nadab	910–909	Evil
Baasha	909–886	Evil
Elah	886–885	Evil
Zimri	885	Evil
Omri	885–874	Evil
Ahab	874–853	Evil
Ahaziah	853–852	Evil
Joram (Jehoram)	852–841	Evil
Jehu	841–814	Evil
Jehoahaz	814–798	Evil
Jehoash (Joash)	798–782	Evil
Jeroboam II	782–753	Evil
Zechariah	753–752	Evil
Shallum	752 (1 month)	Evil
Menahem	752–742	Evil
Pekahiah	742–740	Evil
Pekah	740–732	Evil
Hoshea	732–721	Evil

Judah	Reign	God's Estimate
Rehoboam	931–913 B.C.	Evil
Abijah	913–911	Evil
Asa	911–870	Righteous
Jehoshaphat	870–848	Righteous
Jehoram (Joram)	848–841	Evil
Ahaziah	841	Evil
Athaliah (Queen)	841–835	Evil
Joash	835–796	Evil
Amaziah	796–767	Righteous
Azariah (Uzziah)	767–740	Righteous
Jotham	740–732	Righteous
Ahaz	732–716	Evil
Hezekiah	716–687	Righteous
Manasseh	687–642	Evil
Amon	642–640	Evil
Josiah	640–608	Evil
Jehoahaz	608	Evil
Jehoiakim	609–597	Evil
Jehoiachin	597	Evil
Zedekiah (Mattaniah)	597–586	Evil

The ratio of wicked kings to good kings shows clearly the reason for the final overthrow of both Israel and Judah. With the exception of Shallum, whose reign was too short for appraisal, all the kings of Israel, after the division of the kingdom, are said to have done evil in God's sight. Only six of the twenty kings of Judah are characterized by the expression "he did that which was right in the sight of the Lord." Outstanding among the good kings were Jehoshaphat, Hezekiah (see 2 Ki. 18:13, *note*), and Josiah. Notable among the wicked kings were Ahab and Jeroboam II of Israel, and Manasseh and Jehoiachin of Judah.

In the ninth century B.C., from the reigns of Ahab to Joash in Israel, Elijah and Elisha prophesied (1 Ki. 17:1—2 Ki. 13:20). There were other prophets who lived both in Israel and Judah, among them Joel, Amos, Micah, and Isaiah. They issued warnings against sin and called upon the people of their day to repent. They reminded God's chosen people of His faithfulness in contrast with their unfaithfulness. They predicted that judgment would come upon Israel and Judah. They wept for these nations and pled with them to return to God. Some of their messages were tender, others harsh with judgment. But for the most part their pleas went unheeded. See the introductions in the NSRB to the written messages of these prophets in the books called by their names.

As a guide to the relation of the pre-exilic prophets to their times and the nations with which they were particularly concerned, the following table is presented:

PRE-EXILIC PROPHETS

To Israel		To Judah	
Jonah	c. 800 B.C.	Joel	c. 850–700 B.C.
Amos	c. 780–755		
Hosea	c. 760–710	Hosea	c. 760–710
Micah	c. 740	Micah	c. 740
Nahum	c. 666–615	Isaiah	c. 740–680
		Zephaniah	c. 630–620
		Habakkuk	c. 627–586
		Jeremiah	c. 626–580

In studying the prophetic books in connection with the kingdoms of Israel and Judah, search out the writings directly related

77

to the subject at hand before taking up predictions concerning events of the distant future, such as the first advent of Christ and His second coming and millennial reign. Passages like Isaiah 1:1–23; Jeremiah 5:1–31; Joel 1:1–20; Amos 5:1–17; and Micah 1:1–9 throw light upon God's grief over the unfaithfulness of His people and His righteous judgment which would fall on them.

C. The Captivities

Although there were, as has been stated, some good kings and occasional spiritual revival in Judah, both Israel and Judah suffered spiritual and political decline which ended in submission to Gentile foes and captivity—Israel first and Judah later.

(1) *The northern kingdom—Israel.* It was Assyria that came down against Israel and brought them into captivity. There were two invasions. First, at a date that is imprecise, Pul, known also as Tilgath-pilneser or Tiglath-pileser, invaded the land and took two and a half tribes: Reuben, Gad, and half the tribe of Manasseh (1 Chr. 5:26). At a later date the Assyrians under Shalmaneser defeated and led captive the other seven and a half tribes (2 Ki. 17:1–23; 18:9–12; cp. 2 Ki. 15:19–29; 2 Chr. 28:5–15). This was at the end of the reign of Hoshea as king of Israel, 722–721 B.C. See 2 Chr. 31:21, *note.*

Sometimes people speak of the northern kingdom as the "ten lost tribes." This is a mistake. A substantial number of individuals in the northern kingdom identified themselves with the southern kingdom, the house of David, even before the Assyrian captivity. Thus it appears that all twelve tribes are represented among the Jews. See 2 Ki. 17:23, *note.*

(2) *The southern kingdom—Judah.* After Israel's fall, Judah enjoyed for a short time a period of reform. A revival took place under Hezekiah. Temple worship was restored. Israelites who had escaped captivity united with Judah and reinstituted the Passover Feast with them (2 Ki. 18:1–6; 2 Chr. 29:1—31:21). See 2 Ki. 18:7, *note.*

Manasseh, who succeeded Hezekiah, turned back to idolatry. His long reign of forty-five years and Amon's short one of two or more years was a dark era for Judah. At Amon's death, Josiah ascended the throne and did right in God's sight during his thirty-two-year reign. He restored the Passover, which had been despised and slighted by his two predecessors, but was slain when he met the king of Egypt in a battle near the Euphrates River (2 Chr. 35:20–24). Josiah's four successors were wicked kings. Judah reached its final decline under them and was taken into captivity by Nebuchadnezzar, king of Babylon. There were actually three deportations to Babylon. The first was during the reign of Jehoiakim (Dan. 1:1) about 605 B.C., when Daniel and other princes were deported; the second under Jehoiachin (2 Ki. 24:10–16) in 597 B.C., when 10,000 leading people were taken; and the third when Zedekiah was king (2 Chr. 36:14–21; cp. Ezek. 1:1–4) in 586 B.C., when most of Judah was placed in exile. See Jer. 25:11, *note.*

D. JUDAH RESTORED

There is no record of the ten northern tribes during their captivity. On the other hand, Scripture tells a great deal about the southern kingdom in exile. Daniel offers some information, and portions of Jeremiah and Ezekiel are helpful. But most of the details are found in Ezra, Nehemiah, and Esther.

Nebuchadnezzar, king of Babylon, was not harsh with his captives, whom he seems to have considered more as colonists than slaves. The book of Daniel tells the dramatic story of God's dealings with this great ruler (Dan. 1—4). Succeeding monarchs respected Daniel and were generally kind to their Judean captives (Dan. 5—12)

There were four prophets during Judah's exile:

EXILIC PROPHETS

Jeremiah	c.	626–580 B.C.*
Daniel	c.	605–535
Ezekiel	c.	593–570
Obadiah	c.	585†

*Jeremiah, who is listed among the pre-exilic prophets, entered the captivity.

†Scholars are not agreed about the date of Obadiah. Some place him as early as the ninth century B.C., others as late as the sixth century. The editorial committee of the NSRB agreed on the early part of the sixth century B.C.

Daniel's prophecy, although it includes some historical data relating to Judah, speaks primarily of universal affairs—of kings and kingdoms. Ezekiel, whose writing was not for Judah alone but for "the whole house of Israel" (Ezek. 39:25), reminded a people in exile of the sins that brought them there (e.g. 14:12–23), encouraged them to set their hearts upon their restoration, and looked beyond Judah's experience in his days to the final restoration of all Israel in the distant future. Obadiah's name is unknown apart from his writing. The date of his prophecy is uncertain. But his message of doom, even if it was written specifically about Edom, sounds a note of warning against pride in all people. See the introductions to Ezekiel, Daniel, and Obadiah, NSRB, pp. 838, 896, 939.

After Babylon fell to the Medes and Persians (Dan. 5:30–31; 6:28), Cyrus (Cyrus II or Cyrus the Great, see Isa. 41:2, *note*), king of Persia, gave permission to Judah in exile to return to Jerusalem and rebuild their temple, which had been destroyed by Nebuchadnezzar when he subjugated Judah and Benjamin. The historical record of Judah's restoration is given in Ezra, Nehemiah, and Esther. The writings of two of the three post-exilic prophets also illuminate this period.

POST-EXILIC PROPHETS

Haggai	520 B.C.
Zechariah	520–518
Malachi	c. 450–444

Haggai spoke to a restored remnant of Judah who had procrastinated in rebuilding the temple, rebuking them for their delay and encouraging them to go forward. Zechariah, a contemporary of Haggai, called upon those who were erecting the temple to turn completely to the Lord. He rallied them in their work and told of future days when Messiah would come and reign over a regathered and refined Israel. Malachi wrote after both the temple and the walls of Jerusalem had been rebuilt. His message pointed to the coming of the forerunner of Messiah, that is, John the Baptist. See the introductions to Haggai, Zechariah, and Malachi, NSRB, pp. 961, 964, 978.

Under the edict of Cyrus in 538 B.C., approximately 50,000 people went back to Jerusalem (Ezra 2:64–65). Zerubbabel was their leader. See 1 Chr. 3:19, *note*. He was assisted by Jeshua, a priest also called Joshua, for example Hag. 1:1; Zech. 3:1. The majority of the first expedition was composed of members of the tribe of Judah. With them, however, there were Benjamites and a number of priests and Levites. Furthermore, allusions in the text, such as "the people of Israel" (Ezra 7:13), suggest that some of the northern kingdom who had cast their lot with the house of David made up a part of the expedition. See 2 Ki. 17:23, *note*, par. (3) and (4).

Zerubbabel caused an altar to be set up in Jerusalem and a renewal of sacrifices to the Lord to be established. The erection of the temple met with opposition, but Haggai and Zechariah encouraged Zerubbabel and the people. After about twenty years the work was completed and the Passover Feast restored.

During this interval Babylon had fallen to the Persians and Darius (Darius I Hystaspis, or Darius the Great) had come to the throne of Babylon. For the Persian kings of O.T. times, see Ezra 4:3, *note*; Dan. 11:2, *note* 2. The narrative concerning the first detachment is recorded in Ezra 1—6.

Ezra headed the second expedition of Jews to Jerusalem. This occurred about a half-century after Zerubbabel's emigration, around 455 B.C. Ahasuerus (Est. 1:1), who was in all probability Xerxes, the successor to Darius, died. Artaxerxes (Artaxerxes Longimanus) ascended the throne (Ezra 7:1). At one time he had suspended the rebuilding of the temple. But he relented and wrote a decree which allowed all those who wished to return to Judah to do so. When Ezra arrived in Jerusalem he discovered that many Jews who had come there with the first expedition were mingling with ancient enemies of Israel—Canaanites, Hittites, Ammonites, Moabites, etc. Ezra offered to God prayers of confession on his own part and for the people, and they were reconciled to God. All this is recorded in Ezra 7—10.

The third and last expedition followed ten or eleven years later, in 445 B.C. Nehemiah was its leader. Like Ezra he returned to Jerusalem under Artaxerxes' decree. Through his dynamic leadership the walls were finished in fifty-two days (Neh. 1—7).

Then came a spiritual revival under Ezra. The people repented and fasted, they began to read the law again, and the celebration of the Feast of Tabernacles (Lev. 23:33–36) was restored. Judah, established once more in its land, experienced a period of rest and peace. But the theocracy was not restored. No doubt God was watching over them, but they were inhabitants in Judah and Jerusalem by sufferance of the Gentiles. For the "times of the Gentiles,"* which began when Nebuchadnezzar brought Judah into captivity, will continue until the Lord Jesus Christ, the Messiah of Israel, returns to the earth to reign over it. See Rev. 16:19, *note.*

Malachi was yet to speak to these people about Messiah's forerunner. Then there would be silence until "God, who at sundry times and in diverse manners spoke in time past unto the fathers by the prophets," would speak again "by His Son, whom He hath appointed heir of all things" (Heb. 1:1–2).

*See Ch. XV, p. 145.

CHAPTER IX

Some Important Turning Points in Biblical History: New Testament

THE first turning point recorded in the New Testament is the greatest event in human history—the incarnation of the Son of God. The fall of man radically affected every human being. The return of Christ to the earth to rule the world in righteousness and peace will be a unique event. But the coming of the Son of God into the world overshadows everything else. Though from the beginning God had made Himself known to man, at the incarnation He took on human form—spirit, soul, and body. He lived on earth as man with men. In His real humanity He was physically subject to our limitations (cp. Jn. 4:6) and tempted in every way we are tempted, yet without sinning (Heb. 4:15).

1. God Comes to Earth

Christ's entrance into the world was not an afterthought with God. In the creation of man God endowed him with moral responsibility. Adam and Eve did not need to disobey God, but they did disobey Him as He knew they would. In His foreknowledge, long before man was created, God made provision for him. In the councils of the Godhead—the Father, the Son, and the Holy Spirit—Christ's death for sin was determined (Acts 2:23; 4:27–28; 1 Pet. 1:20). The prophets predicted His birth and His death (e.g. Isa. 7:14; Mic. 5:2; Ps. 22:1–19; Isa. 53:3–12). And while He was on earth Christ Himself spoke of His crucifixion (e.g. Mt. 12:40; 16:21; 17:22–23; 20:17–19).

When Adam and Eve sinned, God provided them with covering for their nakedness, garments made from the skins of slain animals (Gen. 3:21). Abel, the second man born in the world, presented an offering to God which was acceptable to Him. Abel took it from his flock (Gen. 4:4). Noah, when he left the ark, built an altar and there sacrificed animals to God (Gen. 8:20–21). Abraham, in obedience to God, was ready to offer up his son Isaac. He was prevented when God provided a ram in Isaac's place (Gen. 22:1–14). When God gave the law to Moses, He also made provision that every man who broke it should offer a sacrifice for his sins (e.g. Lev. 16:1–4). See Lev. 17:11, *note* 2. This was the divine order for the remission of sin from the earliest days until the coming of Christ and the one perfect and complete offering He made for sin by the sacrifice of Himself (Heb. 9:22, 26; 10:10).

With Christ's death God superseded the covenant He made with Moses with a new covenant. See Mosaic Covenant, Ex. 19:5, *note* 2; New Covenant, Heb. 8:8, *note* 1. The law of Moses did not save men but showed them they were sinners. The sacrifices of Old Testament times did not atone for sin but provided a covering for sin for the time being. See Lev. 16:6, *note*. These were given as a substitute, as it were, until Christ should come and make full atonement by shedding His blood for our sins (Gal. 3:24; 1 Pet. 2:24). Moreover, by His resurrection Christ imparted, through the Holy Spirit, new life to every believer. By faith in Him the sinner is cleansed once and forever (Heb. 10:12), is given power over sin (Rom. 6:14, 18, 22; 8:1–2; Gal. 2:19–20), and is assured of an eternal inheritance with Him in heaven (Heb. 9:15).

In the incarnation the divine promises concerning Israel's Messiah were fulfilled. It was a turning point at which shadows became reality. No longer was God simply *for* man, as salutary as this may be. God was now *with* man (e.g. Immanuel, Isa. 7:14, *marg.*). Animal sacrifices that had to be offered continuously were replaced by the infinite sacrifice at Calvary which redeemed the sinner. The law, which was a symbol of death to the sinner, was supplanted by the Gospel of Christ, which redeems the repentant sinner of whatever race and imparts new life to him by faith. Every spiritual need of man was met when God came down to earth in

84

the Person of His Son and finished His redemptive work on man's behalf.

2. *Pentecost*

"Pentecost" is a transliteration of the Greek word *pentēkostē* meaning *fiftieth*. The day of Pentecost alludes to the Feast of Pentecost, which is also called the Feast of Weeks (Dt. 16:9–10). It was held on the fiftieth day after the Feast of First Fruits. See *notes* at Lev. 23:10, 16. In His resurrection Christ became "the first fruits of them that slept" (1 Cor. 15:20). Forty days after His resurrection the Lord Jesus ascended to heaven (Acts 1:3, 9–10). The tenth day after the ascension, or fifty days after Christ arose, was the day of Pentecost. What happened on this day was a turning point of great significance.

A. THE HOLY SPIRIT GIVEN TO JEWS AND PROSELYTES

The disciples were all gathered together in Jerusalem; for the risen Christ had instructed them not to depart from the city but to "wait for the promise which . . . ye have heard of me" (Acts 1:4; cp. Lk. 24:49; Jn. 14:16, 26; 16:7). It was the Comforter, the Holy Spirit, who was promised. "And when the day of Pentecost was fully come" the waiting disciples "were all filled with the Holy Spirit" (Acts 2:1–4). As a result the followers of the Lord, some of whom had been filled with fear at His crucifixion, became bold witnesses concerning Him. This gift from the Father is the indwelling Spirit of God, the third Person of the Trinity.* He resides within the heart of every believer in Christ (Rom. 8:9). He is the Preserver and Guardian of all Christians.

B. THE HOLY SPIRIT GIVEN TO GENTILES

Not directly related to the day of Pentecost (it is included in this section of this book because it pertains to the gift of the Holy Spirit), is still another turning point in biblical history, namely Peter's visit to the house of Cornelius (Acts 10). Peter addressed a

*See Ch. III, pp. 31f., 36; Ch. XIII, p. 123.

group of Gentiles there, and while he was speaking to them, "the Holy Spirit fell on all them who heard the word" (v. 44). In recounting this experience to Jewish believers in Jerusalem who criticized him for going to the Gentiles, Peter said, "As I began to speak the Holy Spirit fell on them, as on us at the beginning" (Acts 11:15), that is, at Pentecost. No longer was the Gospel reserved for the Jews but it now reached Gentiles as well, as predicted by the prophets and intimated by the Lord Jesus (e.g. Isa. 60:3; Jn. 17:20). It is now clear that during this present age it is the normal thing that the Holy Spirit is given instantly to Jews and Gentiles alike without any condition except their exercise of saving faith in the Lord Jesus Christ. See Acts 10:44, *note*.

3. *The New Testament Church Is Formed*

The Bible nowhere states explicitly that the Church was formed on the day of Pentecost. But that the Church was born with the coming of the Holy Spirit is implicit in more than one passage of Scripture. (Throughout this book, except when quoting directly from Scripture, "church" is spelled with a capital C to distinguish the organism, the mystical body of Christ, the invisible Church, from the organized or local church, the visible church.)

The word "church" is translated from the Greek *ekklēsia* (the root word from which the English "ecclesiastical" is derived) and means *an assemblage, a gathering*. Stephen used the word in a non-technical sense when he stated that Israel was "the church [*lit.* the assemblage] in the wilderness" (Acts 7:38). The same Greek word is translated "assembly" in Acts 19:41, where the town clerk dismissed a crowd gathered to evict Paul from Ephesus. The technical use of *ekklēsia* denotes those who have been called out from the world and gathered together around the Person of Christ (cp. Acts 15:14). In the N.T. context it is perfectly clear whether the word "church" denotes Christ's mystical body or the visible local church.

It is a mistake to confuse the N.T. Church with Israel. The Church did not exist when Christ was on earth. The first mention

86

of the word in the N.T. is in Matthew 16:18 where the Lord Jesus says to Peter, "I will build my church." It is not, as you observe, "I *have built* my church" but "I *will build* my church." The Church was something to be formed in the future.

The Church is said to be the body of Christ. "And He [Christ] is the head of the body, the church" (Col. 1:18; cp. v. 24; Eph. 1:22–23). How does a person become a member of the body of Christ? By baptism with the Holy Spirit. "For by one Spirit are we all baptized into one body, whether we be Jews or Greeks [Gentiles]" (1 Cor. 12:13). When did baptism with the Holy Spirit first take place? At Pentecost. Just before His ascension the risen Christ said to the apostles, "Ye shall be baptized with the Holy Spirit not many days from now" (Acts 1:5). Ten days later, on the day of Pentecost, all of them were baptized with the Spirit (Acts 11:15–17). The filling with the Holy Spirit on the same day (Acts 2:1–4) obviously accompanied baptism with the Spirit and empowered the apostles for service. All believers have been baptized with the Holy Spirit, but not all believers are filled with the Spirit (cp. Eph. 5:18).

4. *A New Age Begins*

With the coming of the Holy Spirit and the formation of the Church a new economy began in God's progressive revelation to man—the sixth dispensation or the Church age. The stewardship of the law, under which the Israelites were placed within a precise discipline of "thou shalt" and "thou shalt not" as a point of testing, ended with the death and resurrection of Christ and the gift of the Holy Spirit. See Fifth Dispensation: the Law, Ex. 19:1, *note*.

Salvation in every dispensation has always been by God's grace through faith. But in the Church age the point of man's testing is his personal faith in the Lord Jesus Christ as his Redeemer. The sinner believes the good news concerning Christ's death and resurrection on his behalf. By faith he is delivered from Satan's domain and translated into the kingdom of the Son of God (Col. 1:13).

During the Church age it is the Christian's responsibility to obey the Lord's command to witness concerning Him everywhere (Mk. 16:15; Acts 1:8). Not everyone who hears the Gospel will receive it. Christ made this clear in His parables of the sower (Mt. 13:3–9, 18–23), and of the wheat and the tares (Mt. 13:24–30, 36–43). But some will believe and be saved. Throughout the age God is calling out a people for His name (Acts 15:14–18). The Church is composed of some Jews and some Gentiles, yet in Christ, that is, in His mystical body, there is no distinction but all are one (Gal. 3:27–29; Eph. 3:5–6). At the same time mankind as a whole is divided into three categories: the Jews, the Gentiles, and the Church of God (1 Cor. 10:32). The Church age will end when the Lord Jesus Christ calls every member of His body, whether he be alive on earth or in the grave, to meet Him in the air to be with Him forever (1 Th. 4:13–18; cp. 1 Cor. 15:51–55). See Sixth Dispensation: the Church, Acts 2:1, *note*.

5. *The Conversion of Saul of Tarsus*

The importance of the conversion of Saul of Tarsus, later called Paul the apostle, can hardly be overemphasized. The record is given in Acts 9:1–31. Paul recounted his experience twice: once to a mob in Jerusalem (Acts 22:1–16) and a second time in his defense before King Agrippa (Acts 26:1–18). The Lord made it clear that Paul was to be God's messenger to the Gentiles (Acts 9:15; 22:21; 26:15–18; cp. Gal. 2:7–8).

Shortly after his conversion Paul went to Arabia (Gal. 1:17), where by direct revelation Jesus Christ made known to him the Gospel of the grace of God. (The Arabian interlude is not mentioned in Acts but is thought to have taken place between verses 21 and 22 of the Acts 9 narrative.) Before Paul went to Arabia he preached that Christ, the Messiah, was the Son of God. Upon his return, although he did not neglect the Jews, he preached with great power in Gentile communities of Asia Minor. The account of his three missionary journeys to predominantly Gentile cities, his arrest, and voyage to Rome comprise the latter half of Acts.

It is not Paul's missionary service, however, but his ministry to the Church, especially in his letters, that makes the conversion of Paul so vital. More fully than any other N.T. writer the Apostle Paul develops the doctrine of the Church. Not only does he speak of the administration of local churches, but he also expounds the basis of the believer's redemption, justification, sanctification, and glorification. Christ taught His disciples the oneness of His people (Jn. 17:21–23). But the doctrine of the unity of believers among themselves and with the Father, Son, and Holy Spirit is revealed still more fully in the Pauline epistles. The Church as the body of Christ was a secret which had been hidden in God from creation (Eph. 3:1–12). Paul was ordained by the Lord to make all men see this truth. The Church (both mystical and visible) would be poorer, in fact the Church would be deprived of a great many treasures of the unsearchable riches of Christ, were it not for the epistles of Paul. See The Epistles of Paul, NSRB, p. 1209.

6. *Some Future Turning Points*

There are other turning points yet to come in the record of biblical history, since in God's Word all time—past, present, and future—is unrolled like a scroll in the span between two eternities. Some important turning points of the future—the translation of the Church from earth to heaven, the judgment seat of Christ, the period of tribulation that will come on the earth, the return of Christ to the earth, the millennial kingdom, the judgment of the great white throne, and the eternal state—are subjects of another chapter.*

*Ch. XV.

CHAPTER X

The Christ Event

IN type, in prophecy, and in history Christ is the theme of all Scripture. In the earliest pages of the Bible His coming to earth as the seed of the woman is predicted (Gen. 3:15). The sacrifices of the tabernacle and temple were types or figures representing Him and His work. See *notes* at Gen. 2:23; cp. *notes* at Lev. 16:5; 17:11; also NSRB, Index, p. 1381, "CHRIST, types of," for locations of *notes* on various types of Christ. His pre-existence is presented, as well as the nature and place of His birth as the incarnate Son of God (Isa. 7:14; see Mic. 5:2, *note*). Prophecies abound in the Old Testament concerning an earthly kingdom over which Christ will reign. A familiar one is found in Isaiah 9:6–7: "For unto us a child is born, unto us a son is given, and the government shall be upon his shoulder; and his name shall be called Wonderful, Counselor, The Mighty God, The Everlasting Father [*or* Father of the Ages], The Prince of Peace. Of the increase of his government and peace there shall be no end, upon the throne of David, and upon his kingdom, to order it, and to establish it with justice and righteousness from henceforth even forever. The zeal of the Lord of hosts will perform this." In the Psalms and prophetic writings Christ's death is foretold. Psalm 22 and Isaiah 53 illustrate this. See *notes* at Ps. 22:7; Isa. 53:9. To read the O.T. without looking for and finding Christ in its pages is to miss its major message.

"Christ" (Gk. *Christós*) means *anointed*. Its counterpart is "Messiah" (Heb. *mâshîach*; Gk. *Messías*). Christ is the New Testament name of the O.T. Messiah—the Anointed One. Jesus Christ is Jesus the Messiah. Jesus is the human name of the Son of God. Christ is His official name. See Mt. 1:16, *note* 2. His full title is the Lord Jesus Christ.

1. *The Birth of Christ*

The birth of Jesus Christ was a miracle. Centuries before Jesus was born His virgin birth was predicted. At the time He was conceived it was reaffirmed.

Although in the natural process of birth the seed or sperm emanates from the male, in Eden God said that there would be enmity between the serpent's seed and the woman's seed. In the eighth century B.C. the Lord gave a sign, not only to Ahaz but to the house of David as well, saying, "Behold, the virgin shall conceive, and bear a son, and his name shall be called Immanuel [meaning *God with us*]" (Isa. 7:14). At the time of Christ's conception the Angel Gabriel told Mary, who had never known a man intimately (Mt. 1:18, 25; Lk. 1:34), that she would conceive and bear a son. This was in confirmation of Isaiah's prophecy that "the virgin should be with child" (Mt. 1:22–23).*

Jesus Christ had no human father. He was conceived in Mary by the Holy Spirit, as Gabriel told her: "The Holy Spirit shall come upon thee, and the power of the Highest shall overshadow thee; therefore also that holy thing which shall be born of thee shall be called the Son of God" (Lk. 1:35).

For information concerning the two genealogies of Jesus (Mt. 1:1–17; Lk. 3:23–38), see Lk. 3:23 *note*; cp. Mt. 1:11, *note*.

2. *Christ's Baptism*

Preparatory to beginning His public ministry, Christ was baptized in the Jordan River by John the Baptist (Mt. 3:13–17; Mk. 1:9–11; Lk. 3:21–22; cp. Jn. 1:29–34).

---

*The Hebrew word *'almâh*, rendered "virgin" in Isaiah 7:14, is used six other times in the O.T. It is translated "virgin" (Gen. 24:43), "virgins" (Song 1:3; 6:8), "damsels" (Ps. 68:25), "maid" (Ex.2:8; Prov. 30:19). In no instance does the context suggest a married woman. *Parthénos* is the Greek word for "virgin." Citing Isaiah 7:14, Matthew writes, "Behold, the virgin [*parthénos*] shall be with child, and shall bring forth a son, and they shall call his name Immanuel, which, being interpreted, is God with us" (Mt. 1:23). In such a way the Holy Spirit confirmed that Isaiah's distant prediction was related to Christ's virgin birth.

Some have wondered why Jesus submitted to baptism, since John baptized "unto repentance" (Mt. 3:11). John himself was puzzled about it (v. 14). Through His baptism by John, Christ identified Himself with those He came to save (Mt. 1:21), John identified Him as the Lamb of God, the Sin-Bearer (Jn. 1:29), and God the Father and God the Holy Spirit identified Him as the Son of God (Mt. 3:16–17). See Mt. 3:15, *note*.

On the occasion of Christ's baptism the divine Trinity, implied in the O.T. (cp. Gen. 1:2; Ps. 90:2; Mic. 5:2), was manifested together for the first time. See *notes* at Mt. 3:16; 28:19.

3. Christ's Temptation

Matthew and Luke give full accounts of Christ's temptation (Mt. 4:1–11; Lk. 4:1–13). Mark mentions it in two sentences (Mk. 1:12–13). Jesus fasted in the wilderness for forty days and nights (Mt. 4:2). His temptation lasted during the full forty days (Mk. 1:13; Lk. 4:2).

Satan's purpose in tempting the Lord Jesus was to induce Him to act independently of God the Father: to turn stones into bread and thus satisfy His human need in a supernatural way (Mt. 4:3), to make a public display of His divine power as a means of avoiding the cross (vv. 5–6), and to worship the devil rather than the Father in heaven (vv. 8–9). In each instance Jesus rejected the temptation by resorting to the Scriptures (vv. 4, 7, 10; cp. Dt. 8:3; 6:16; 10:20).

Christ, who came to do the Father's will (Heb. 10:7,9; cp. Ps. 40:7–8; Jn. 8:29), could not be seduced by Satan's devices. He was tempted in all points as we are tempted, but He did not sin (Heb. 4:15). The same shield that He used for thwarting the tempter—faith in the Word of God—is at our disposal also. See Mt. 4:1, *note*.

Because Jesus Christ was born of a virgin He did not inherit a sinful nature such as every other person born into this world possesses. It is inconceivable that God the Son could sin. He was "holy, harmless, undefiled, [and] separate from sinners" (Heb.

7:26). He "knew no sin" (2 Cor. 5:21). There was nothing in Him to which sin could attach itself. He "did no sin, neither was guile found in his mouth" (1 Pet. 2:22). When He asked some who opposed Him, "Which of you convicteth me of sin?" (Jn. 8:46), none could accuse Him. The Lamb of God who came to take away the sin of the world was, like the animal sacrifices of O.T. times, "without blemish and without spot" (1 Pet. 1:19). It was because He Himself had never sinned and could not sin that He was able to bear our sins in His body when He died vicariously at Calvary.

4. Christ's Kingdom Message

There are two phases of Christ's kingdom message. First He addressed Himself to the Jews. Then His message went out to men and women of every nation. See Mt. 4:17, *note* 3.

A. The Kingdom Presented and Rejected

After Jesus' baptism by John and His temptation by the devil (Mt. 3:13—4:11), He "began to preach and to say, Repent, for the kingdom of heaven is at hand" (Mt. 4:17). This is the same message that Messiah's forerunner, John the Baptist, had given earlier (Mt. 3:2). Now the King Himself was among His people proclaiming that the kingdom was at hand.

God promised David an everlasting kingdom on earth (2 Sam. 7:8-16). See Davidic Covenant, 2 Sam. 7:16, *note*. Among other prophets, Jeremiah spoke of this Davidic kingdom (Jer. 23:5-6). Ezekiel predicted it (Ezek. 37:24-28). Hosea also mentioned it (Hos. 3:4-5). Certainly there must have been many in Israel when the Lord Jesus began His work on earth, who were looking for the Messiah. But evidently their thoughts and hopes were focused on His coming in irresistible power to judge their oppressors. Such expressions as these must have been in their minds: "Thou shalt break them with a rod of iron" (Ps. 2:9); "Our God shall come, and shall not keep silence; a fire shall devour before him, and it shall be very tempestuous round about him" (Ps. 50:3); and, "Yet once, it is a little while, and I will shake the heavens . . . and I will shake all nations" (Hag. 2:6–7). So when One, who seemed to them a humble Galilean peasant, announced that the kingdom of heaven was at hand, and proposed in a speech given on a hilltop that the principles of that kingdom offered special happiness to the poor in spirit, the meek, the hungry, the peacemakers, and those who would be persecuted, and that the heirs of the kingdom should not resist evil but should love their enemies, the religious leaders and the majority of the Jews of His time rejected Him and His message. He came to His own things—the world He created and His creatures—and His own people did not receive Him (Jn. 1:11).

"At hand," as the expression is used in the N.T., does not necessarily mean immediacy but, rather, imminence. For example, Peter wrote, "The end of all things is at hand" (1 Pet. 4:7). The end could come at any time. Compare Rom. 13:12; Phil. 4:5; Rev. 1:3; 22:10. See Mt. 4:17, *note 4*.

Certainly the offer of the kingdom was genuine. God would not mock His people. In His foreknowledge, however, God knew what Israel would do. There is no point in speculating what would have happened *if* Israel had accepted Christ and the kingdom at this time. Divine foreknowledge implies more than God's knowing something before it takes place. It also involves His purposes. God is sovereign. His program for the world is not dependent upon the whims of His creatures or on any other fluctuating circumstances, but upon His eternal intent.

Furthermore—and this is of supreme importance—the prophets predicted not only Messiah's rejection but also that He would die for the sins of His people. "He is despised and rejected of men . . . he was wounded for our transgressions . . . the LORD hath laid on Him the iniquity of us all. . . . For he was cut out of the land of the living; for the transgression of my people was he stricken. And he made his grave with the wicked" (Isa. 53:5–6, 8–9; cp. Ps. 22; Dan. 9:25–26). The trustworthiness of the Scriptures, in fact the integrity of God Himself, demanded that Christ should be crucified. The leaders of Israel in Christ's time seem to have had no understanding of this phase of His work. And although He reminded His disciples about it on several occasions, they too did not understand it (Lk. 18:31–34; cp. Mt. 16:21–22; 17:22–24). Yet the Son of man came "to give his life a ransom for many" (Mt. 20:28).

The official rejection of the King took place at a later date, when the chief priests and elders of the Jews demanded of Pilate, "Crucify him!" (Mt. 27:20–25; Mk. 15:11–14). The fact of this rejection became apparent when He was repudiated in certain key cities where He had performed miracles. Therefore He began to speak of their judgment (Mt. 11:20–24). At the same time He began to preach a new message addressed to individuals in every nation, Gentiles as well as Jews: "Come unto me, all ye that labor and are heavy laden, and I will give you rest" (Mt. 11:28; cp. 12:50; 16:25). See *notes* at Mt. 11:20, 28. Yet the kingdom of heaven was still at hand—the kingdom of heaven in a form that had been hidden in God from the foundation of the world (Mt. 13:34–35). Christ Himself revealed it, but its full course and role on earth would not go into effect until after His death and resurrection. See Mt. 3:2, *note*.

B. The Kingdom in Mystery Form

After He invited all people in need, whoever they were, to come to Him for rest, the Lord Jesus experienced further opposition from the religious leaders. The Pharisees accused Him and His disciples of breaking the law of Moses when they plucked ears of grain on the sabbath day (Mt. 12:1–2). Because He healed a paralytic in the synagogue on the sabbath, the Pharisees met together to discover a way to destroy Him (Mt. 12:9–14). Jesus withdrew from them and reached out to the multitudes. Matthew reminds his readers that this was in fulfillment of Isaiah's prophecy concerning the Son of God, "Behold my servant whom I have chosen, my beloved, in whom my soul is well pleased; I will put my Spirit upon him, and he shall show justice to the Gentiles . . . and in his name shall the Gentiles trust" (Mt. 12:17–21; cp. Isa. 42:1–4; Amos 9:11–12). See *notes* at Isa. 42:1; Mt. 12:18.

It was not long after this that Christ unveiled, in a series of seven parables recorded in Matthew 13, a secret that had never before been revealed—the progress of the Gospel in the present age. The Lord spoke of these parables as "the mysteries of the kingdom of heaven" (v. 11).

A parable is a kind of simile, a likening of one thing to another in order to throw light upon a certain truth. Jesus made liberal use of parables in His teaching, employing terms familiar to His audiences—grain and earth, leaven and dough, coins and treasures, sheep and fishnets—to illustrate great spiritual principles. See Lk. 21:29, *note*.

A "mystery" in Scripture is not some truth that is concealed and can only be discovered by intelligent investigation. It is a truth that, until the occasion of its announcement, has been hidden but is now being divinely revealed. For instance, Paul says, "Behold, I show [make known to] you a mystery: We shall not all sleep, but we shall all be changed" (1 Cor. 15:51). The fact that a generation of believers in Christ will not die physically but will one day be changed from men and women with corruptible bodies into beings with incorruptible spiritual bodies was not disclosed until Paul wrote his letters (cp. 1 Th. 4:13–18). For the other ten N.T. mysteries, see Mt. 13:11, *note*.

Christ introduced the kingdom of heaven in its mystery form with the parable of the sower and the soils (Mt. 13:3–9). Here a man sows seed. Some seed falls by the wayside and is devoured by birds (v. 4). Some falls on stony ground and yields grain almost immediately, but is scorched by the sun because the roots have no depth (vv. 5–6). Some falls among thorns and its growth is choked (v. 7). Other seed falls into good soil and yields plentifully (v. 8).

The Lord Himself interpreted this parable (vv. 18–23). The Son of man is the sower (cp. v. 37). The seed He sows is the Word. The soil signifies human hearts, which are likened to shallow soil, stony ground, thorny areas, and good soil. The wicked one, Satan, catches away the first; trials stifle the growth of the second; fondness for the world and its attractions chokes the Word of the third. But that same Word of God falls into receptive hearts and is fruitful. Three-fourths of the seed sown does not result in lasting growth. Only one-fourth bears fruit, and that in varying degrees. See Mt. 13:3, *note* 4.

The second parable of Matthew 13 begins, "The kingdom of heaven is likened unto a man who sowed good seed in his field; but while men slept his enemy came and sowed tares among the wheat, and went his way" (vv. 24–25). When the wheat began to grow, tares (or weeds) appeared. The servants wanted to gather up the weeds, but the owner of the field told them to wait until the harvest; otherwise they might pull up wheat with weeds.

Christ interpreted this parable also (vv. 36–43). He identified the sower as the Son of man (a name Christ frequently employed of Himself; see Mt. 8:20, *note*). He designated the field as the world, the good seed as children of the kingdom, the weeds as children of the devil, the servants as angels, and the harvest as the end of the age. At the end of the age the angels will gather out of this kingdom all offenders, children of the devil (cp. Jn. 8:44; 1 Jn. 3:8–10), and cast them into the lake of fire. The righteous, children of the kingdom, will "shine forth as the sun in the kingdom of their Father" (Mt. 13:43). See *notes* at Mt. 13:24, 43.

It is clear, from the first two parables, that the kingdom of heaven in its mystery form is not the Davidic kingdom; for the Davidic kingdom was made known in O.T. times, whereas the kingdom in mystery form had been "kept secret from the foundation of the world" (vv. 34–35). Nor is it heaven, for Satan will not take anyone away from there, nor will any of his children be there. Neither is it the true Church, the mystical body of Christ. There are no children of the devil in the true Church. The kingdom in mystery is Christendom, that portion of the world where the name of Christ is professed. It is the visible church, composed of unbelievers as well as believers, that constitutes the kingdom of heaven in mystery. It will continue till the end of the age, when Christ will return to the earth to reign as King.

To interpret the five remaining parables of this series, follow the Lord's interpretation of the first two. If the sower in the

97

parable of the tares among the wheat is the Son of man, the Son of man is also the sower in the parable of the sower and the soils. If the field is the world in the second parable, it is the world in the third and fifth parables. If the man of the second parable is the Son of man, He is also the man in parables three, five, and six. If the seed is the Word in the first parable, then it is the Word, or that which the sowing of the Word produces, in the third parable. When figurative words, which are not explained by the Lord Jesus, are employed, compare their use in other Scriptures as a key to interpretation. See *notes* at Mt. 13:31, 33, 44, 45, 47.

Christ made use of further parabolic teaching to instruct His followers about the kingdom of heaven (Mt. 18:23–35; 20:1–16; 22:1–14; 25:1–30). These five parables are not designated as being among the "mysteries of the kingdom of heaven." They refer, not to this present time but to that which will follow after this age. They must be interpreted in their context and under the principles established in Christ's explanations of the first two parables of Matthew 13.

C. The Messianic Kingdom

Christ spoke also of His earthly reign on the throne of His father, David. This period is known as the Messianic kingdom, the Davidic kingdom, and the millennial kingdom. He mentioned this reign in His Olivet Discourse, where He alluded to His return to the earth in glory (Mt. 25:31–46). Before Him all nations will be gathered. The sheep will be assembled on His right hand. On His left hand the goats will be gathered. To the former the King will say, "Come, ye blessed of my Father, inherit the kingdom prepared for you from the foundation of the world" (v. 34). To those on His left hand He will pronounce judgment, "Depart from me . . . into everlasting fire" (v. 41). See Mt. 25:32, *note*. This will be the initial act of the righteous earthly reign of David's greater Son.*

*For a discussion of the millennial kingdom, see Ch. XV, p. 151ff.

5. *Christ's Redemptive Message*

One of the purposes of the incarnation of the Son of God was, as the Angel Gabriel told Joseph, that He should "save his people from their sins" (Mt. 1:21).* Christ Himself confirmed the angelic pronouncement when He said, "The Son of man is come to save that which was lost" (Mt. 18:11; cp. Lk. 19:10). Christ did not come to judge the world (though He *will* judge it, Jn. 5:22), but to save the world (Jn. 12:47; cp. Lk. 9:56). God's method for accomplishing this was that His Son should die for the sins of the world, should "give his life a ransom for many" (Mt. 20:28; Mk. 10:45; cp. Jn. 3:17). These few citations from Christ's own message about His redemptive mission make it clear that the reason for His coming to the earth was constantly on His mind.

A. He Offers Forgiveness

Men can forgive those who have sinned against them. Only God can forgive sins against Himself. On one occasion, when Jesus was in Capernaum, some friends of a paralyzed man brought him to Jesus. The Lord said to the paralytic, "Son, thy sins are forgiven thee." Some of the scribes who were there reasoned, "Why doth this man thus speak blasphemies? Who can forgive sins but God only?" Christ replied that it was just as easy to say "Your sins are forgiven" as to tell a paralyzed man to get up and walk. "But that ye may know that the Son of man hath authority on earth to forgive sins (he saith to the sick of the palsy), I say unto thee, Arise, and take up thy bed, and go thy way unto thine own house." Immediately the paralytic did so. (Mk. 2:1–12; cp. Lk. 7:40–50).

---

*Some other purposes of the incarnation were that Christ should reveal the Father to men (Mt. 11:27; cp. Jn. 1:18; 14:9), do the Father's will (Heb. 10:7, 9), destroy the devil and his works (Heb. 2:14; 1 Jn. 3:8), put away sin (Heb. 9:26; 1 Jn. 3:5; cp. Jn. 1:29), and announce and offer His kingdom over which He will reign (Mt. 4:17; Lk. 1:31–33).

"Forgive," which is synonymous with "remit," means literally *to send away*. In forgiving a sinner, God sends away his sins. The sinner and his sins are thus separated. Even a believer in Christ needs divine forgiveness, since a redeemed sinner does not live sinlessly. When he sins, his fellowship with God is broken. But when he confesses that sin, God forgives him (1 Jn. 1:9), separating the sin from the sinner and bringing the sinner back into complete fellowship with Himself. See Mt. 26:28, *note*. God's forgiveness, no matter what the circumstances may be, is through Christ's sacrifice for sin at Calvary. For "without shedding of blood is no remission" (Heb. 9:22; cp. 1 Jn. 1:7).

The Christian is expected to forgive the sins of his fellow men. If he does not, God will not forgive him (Mt. 6:14-15; cp. v. 12; Eph. 4:32). See Mt. 6:12, *note*.

B. He Offers New Life

Divine forgiveness brings salvation to the sinner. Salvation involves new life among other things. See Rom. 1:16, *note*. Jesus said to Nicodemus, "Except a man be born again [i.e. from above] he cannot see the kingdom of God. Except a man be born of water and of the Spirit, he cannot enter the kingdom of God" (Jn. 3:3,5).

To be born again is to receive new life. "That which is born of the flesh is flesh," Christ said, "and that which is born of the Spirit is spirit" (Jn. 3:6; cp. Jn. 1:13). The new life the believer receives is the life of Christ Himself, whose Spirit resides within regenerated men and women (Gal. 2:20; Col. 1:27; cp. Rom. 8:9-10). This life, as He said many times, is everlasting or eternal (Jn. 3:15; 5:24; 6:27, 40; 10:28; 12:49-50; 17:2-3). Eternal life denotes more than quantity of life, more than duration; it signifies quality of life, life that is abundant and divine (Jn. 10:10). It is a present possession as well as a future hope. It speaks of everlasting fellowship with God through Jesus Christ. See Rev. 22:19, *note*.

Those who are perishing because they do not believe on Jesus Christ as the Son of God will be judged forever (Mt. 25:46;

Jn. 3:36). Their end is not annihilation but spiritual death (cp. 2 Th. 1:8–9). They will experience duration of existence, but they will not possess the divine life which God bestows. This is the second death—separation from God eternally. See Rev. 20:14, *note*.

C. He Requires Faith

Faith, in its N.T. usage, consists in believing what God says, and of receiving it personally. For faith to be effective there must be a response in the heart and an act of the will in regard to the divine revelation or provision made. "Faith" is synonymous with "belief" and "trust." See Jn. 3:16, *note* 1; Heb. 11:39, *note*.

John's Gospel is filled with statements by Christ concerning faith's part in man's salvation. A few examples will substantiate this. "As Moses lifted up the serpent in the wilderness, even so must the Son of man be lifted up, that whosoever believeth in him should not perish, but have eternal life" (Jn. 3:15). "Verily, verily, I say unto you, He that believeth on me hath everlasting life" (Jn. 6:47). To those who inquired what they should do to accomplish the works of God, Jesus replied, "This is the work of God, that ye believe on him whom he hath sent" (Jn. 6:29).

The faith that God requires of us, then, is not just mental assent to a set of facts about Christ, but belief in a Person—Jesus Christ, the Son of God. To trust Him is to trust God. Forgiveness, salvation, and new life which is eternal are offered to all who believe on the Lord Jesus Christ.

6. *Christ's Many Other Words*

Just as Christ did many things not recorded in the Gospels (Jn. 20:30; 21:25), so He must have said many things that are not written there. For instance, Paul told the Ephesian elders "to remember the words of the Lord Jesus, how he said, It is more blessed to give than to receive" (Acts 20:35). While such teaching may be implicit in some of Christ's words, it is not in the four Gospels.

A. His Comforting Words

Christ has a message for every anguished soul. Among His comforting words are these: "Come unto me . . . and I will give you rest" (Mt. 11:28). "If any man thirst, let him come unto me, and drink" (Jn. 7:37). "I am the good shepherd" (Jn. 10:11; see Jn. 10:7, *note*). "I am the resurrection, and the life. . . . And whosoever liveth and believeth in me shall never die" (Jn. 11:25–26). "Let not your heart be troubled, neither let it be afraid" (Jn. 14:27).

B. His Stern Words

Jesus did not hesitate to speak severely against hyprocrisy and sin of every kind. Furthermore, He declared unequivocally that eternal judgment will fall on those who reject Him. It would be difficult to find anywhere in literature stronger denunciation than Christ pronounced over the scribes and Pharisees (see Mt. 2:4, *note*; Mt. 3:7, *note* 1) shortly before His trial and death. "Woe unto you, scribes and Pharisees, hypocrites! For ye compass sea and land to make one proselyte, and when he is made, ye make him twofold more a child of hell than yourselves" (Mt. 23:15). See Mt. 23:2, *note* 3. "If you believe not that I am he [the Son of God], ye shall die in your sins" (Jn. 8:24).

C. His Prophetic Words

Prophecy consists not only in predictions of things to come but also in declaring God's message concerning life and conduct. See *notes* at Dt. 13:4; 1 Cor. 12:10. Christ was a prophet who possessed prophetic credentials without any limitation. See Lk. 24:19, *note*. Regarding His utterances of predictive prophecy, it has already been shown that, in the mystery parables of Matthew 13, Christ prophesied concerning the course of this present age. In His Olivet Discourse (Mt. 24—25), Jesus gave the pattern of events that will take place at the very end of this age when He comes in power.* And before His ascension into heaven He

*See Ch. XV, p. 147.

predicted that the Father's promise of the Holy Spirit would soon occur (Lk. 24:49; Acts 1:4). This was fulfilled at the advent of the Spirit at Pentecost (Acts 2:1-4).

D. HIS WORDS OF WISDOM

Christ spoke with authority (Mt. 7:29; Mk. 1:27). "His word was with power" (Lk. 4:32). He also spoke with great wisdom (1 Cor. 1:30). Those who heard Him could not help but recognize this. "From where hath this man this wisdom?" they asked (Mt. 13:54). It was with divine wisdom that He put to silence the questions of His opponents when they tried to trap Him. A prime example of this was His reply to the Pharisees and Herodians (see Mt. 22:16, *note*) who inquired of Him whether it was lawful for them, as Jews, to pay tribute to Caesar (Lk. 20:19-26). On another occasion Christ was asked by the Sadducees (see Mt. 3:7, *note* 2) about seven brothers who died, each having had in succession the same woman as his wife. Whose wife would she be in the resurrection? Jesus' answer not only silenced them but, from that time, they did not dare question Him any more (Lk. 20:27-40; cp. Mt. 22:23-33, where see *note* at v. 29).

"Never man spoke like this man" (Jn. 7:46). Only by repeated reading of Christ's words, and thoughtful meditation on them, do we really begin to see their depths of meaning.

7. Christ's Miracles

A miracle is a display of supernatural power, normal with God but contrary to nature as we know it. Divine miracles were performed to show forth the glory of God and to fulfill His purposes. They occur in both the O.T. and the N.T. Miracles are also called signs, wonders, and mighty works (Ex. 4:17, 21; Isa. 7:14; Jer. 32:21; Mt. 14:2; Lk. 11:30; Jn. 4:48; 5:20; 20:30; Acts 2:22; Rom. 15:19). Miracles cannot be rationalized, else they would not be miracles. They are accepted in faith.

In O.T. times God sometimes acted directly, without any human agency (Ex. 16:4; Isa. 38:7-8). On other occasions He employed men as His agents (e.g. Moses, Ex. 14:15-16, 21; Elijah, 1 Ki. 18:17-40; Elisha, 2 Ki. 4:32-37).

In N.T. times Christ was the chief miracle worker. In contrast with other men, He acted in His own power to perform signs and wonders (Mt. 9:6; cp. Mt. 28:18; Jn. 10:18); for He is God. Some of the apostles were given miraculous power also (e.g. Peter, Acts 3:1-8; Paul, Acts 28:7-8). God also exercised His power in miraculous ways independent of human instruments, as when "the veil of the temple was torn in two from the top to the bottom" (Mk. 15:38).

Both in the O.T. and the N.T. the divine use of human agents in the performance of miracles attests the validity of their witness. See Acts 28:8, *note*. Even in the case of Christ, His mighty works were employed by the Holy Spirit to reveal His Person (Jn 10:37-38).

A. Christ's Miracles in the Human Realm

Jesus was a man of great compassion. He did miraculous works on behalf of people, not only when they had physical infirmities or were overwhelmed with grief but also when He saw their material and spiritual lack. His compassion moved Him to heal the sick (Mt. 14:14), restore sight to the blind (Mt. 20:34), cure lepers (Mk. 1:41), and even raise the dead (Lk. 7:13-14). The Gospels are filled with Jesus' miracles of healing and restoration. But His greatest miracle on mankind's behalf was and is in giving new life to those who, dead in trespasses and sins, believe on Him.

The signs and wonders Christ did brought glory to God (Mt. 9:8; 15:31; Lk. 13:13; 17:15). They showed that He was who He claimed to be (Mt. 11:2-6; 14:31-33; cp. Jn. 9:1-38).

B. His Miracles in the Realm of Nature

God has ordered the laws of nature. Christ, the Creator (Jn. 1:3; Col. 1:16; Heb. 1:2), is not limited by them but may intervene at any time for His own purposes. See Isa. 38:8, *note*.

This He did on a number of occasions. By His miraculous power He turned water into wine (Jn. 2:1–11), multiplied fish and loaves of bread (Mt. 14:15–21; 15:32–38), caused a fish to swallow a coin (Mt. 17:24–27), and walked on water (Mk. 6:45–51). Moreover He showed, when He quieted the winds and the sea (Mt. 8:23–27), that He controls the elements (cp. Col. 1:17). No wonder men marveled at His power (Mk. 4:41; 6:51)!

C. His Miracles Beyond the Realm of Nature

Christ did mighty works in the spiritual realm also. Demons were subject to Him (Mt. 8:28–32; 12:22). Still other miracles involve His own Person—His transfiguration, resurrection, and ascension.

8. Christ's Transfiguration

One of the most astounding phenomena that took place in the earthly life of the Lord Jesus Christ was His transfiguration. All three Synoptic Gospels carry an account of it (Mt. 16:28—17:9; Mk. 9:1–9; Lk. 9:27–36).

The narratives are clear. Jesus took three of His disciples—Peter, James, and John—up a mountain. "And he was transfigured before them" (Mt. 17:2; Mk. 9:2). The word rendered "transfigured" (Gk. *metamorphóō*, from which our English word "metamorphosis" is derived) is used only two other times in the N.T. It is translated "changed"—"But we all . . . are changed from glory to glory" (2 Cor. 3:18)—and "transformed"—"And . . . be ye transformed by the renewing of your mind" (Rom. 12:2). It means *to change in form*. Luke says "the appearance of his countenance was altered" (Lk. 9:29). The Lord's face shone like the sun and His garments were as white as the light. At the same time Moses and Elijah, men who had lived on earth centuries before Christ, appeared with Him on the mountaintop. Luke reveals the subject of their conversation: Christ's "decease [*lit.* exodus] which he should accomplish at Jerusalem" (Lk. 9:31).

The three disciples were frightened at what took place. Then a cloud overshadowed Christ, Moses, and Elijah, and from it the voice of God the Father said, "This is my beloved Son, in whom I am well pleased; hear ye him" (Mt. 17:5; cp. 3:17).

When the cloud was gone, the disciples saw only Jesus, who was no longer transfigured as He was a few moments before. He instructed them to tell no one what they had seen, until after He was raised from the dead. They obeyed Him. But they never forgot the experience. Around thirty-five years later Peter wrote that he had been an eyewitness of the power and coming of the Lord Jesus Christ. "For," he said, "he [Christ] received from God the Father honor and glory, when there came such a voice from the excellent glory, This is my beloved Son, in whom I am well pleased. And this voice which came from heaven we heard, when we were with him in the holy mount" (2 Pet. 1:16–18).

Peter, James, and John saw in this mountaintop experience "the Son of man coming in his kingdom" (Mt. 16:28). They gazed upon a scene that offered a foreview of what will take place when He returns to the earth to reign. (1) The Lord appeared in visible glory (Rev. 19:11–13,16; cp. Mt. 25:31); (2) Moses was with Him as a symbol of those who will have passed through death and will return to earth with Him (Jude 14); and (3) Elijah, who never died but was caught up to heaven in a whirlwind (2 Ki. 2:11), was there as a figure of God's people who will have been translated to heaven without dying, whom the Lord will bring with Him when He comes again to establish His kingdom (1 Th. 4:13–17; cp. 1 Cor. 15:51–52). See Mt. 17:2, *note*.

The presence on the holy mount of Moses and Elijah with Christ gave the three disciples evidence that both the law (Moses) and the prophets (Elijah) bear witness that Jesus Christ is the Son of God and that He will surely come in power and glory to rule this earth.

9. *Christ's Prayers*

Jesus, with His twelve disciples, had commemorated His last Passover. See *notes* at Ex. 12:11; Lev. 23:5. During this feast Judas departed. Jesus then instituted the Lord's Supper. He and the eleven left the upper room and walked toward the Mount of Olives. His hour had come. In the Garden of Gethsemane He went aside by Himself, fell down on His face before God, and prayed, "Father, if thou be willing, remove this cup from me; nevertheless, not my will, but thine, be done" (Lk. 22:42).

Why should God pray to God? Because, although Christ was indeed God, He was also truly man. In His humanity He was as dependent upon God the Father as any other man. This is a mystery, but it is so.

A. Some Occasions of Christ's Prayers

Jesus Christ was a man of prayer. At His baptism, He prayed (Lk. 3:21). During His first tour of Galilee, Mark says of Him, "And in the morning, rising up a great while before day, he went out, and departed into a solitary place, and there prayed" (Mk. 1:35). After He miraculously cleansed a leper, Jesus "withdrew himself into the wilderness, and prayed" (Lk. 5:16). When He was about to choose the Twelve, "he went out into a mountain to pray, and continued all night in prayer to God" (Lk. 6:12). Before He walked on the Sea of Galilee, He spent time in prayer (Mk. 6:46). Between the time that our Lord fed the five thousand and Peter's great confession concerning Him, "he was praying" (Lk. 9:18). It was "as he prayed" that Jesus was transfigured before Peter, James, and John (Lk. 9:29). Christ promised His disciples that he would pray to His Father to send the Holy Spirit to abide with them forever (Jn. 14:16), and He told Peter that He had prayed for him, so that his faith would not fail (Lk. 22:31–32).

B. An Example of Christ's Prayers

John 17 records what is generally known as Christ's high-priestly prayer or His intercessory prayer. It is the Lord's own prayer. What is traditionally called The Lord's Prayer is, of course, a model prayer which Jesus taught His followers (Mt. 6:9–13; Lk. 11:1–4, where see *note* at v. 2).

The prayer in John 17 was made somewhere along the way to the Mount of Olives. Jesus "lifted up his eyes to heaven, and said, Father, the hour is come; glorify thy Son, that thy Son also may glorify thee" (v. 1). The prayer was intimate and direct. It speaks of the Son's work on earth and of His relationships with His followers—those whom the Father had entrusted to Him, and those who would believe in Him in future days. See *notes* at Jn. 17:1, 2.

Observe that the Lord's own prayer of John 17 follows in several ways the pattern of prayer that He taught His disciples. (1) It is addressed to the Father (v. 1); (2) it begins by ascribing glory to God (vv. 1–4); (3) it places the program of God as of first importance (v. 5); and (4) it relates to the personal needs of the petitioner and others of God's people, and intercedes on their behalf (vv. 6–26).

C. Christ's Submissiveness in His Prayers

Jesus and His eleven disciples were in Gethsemane. His betrayal and arrest were hardly more than moments away. He knew that He was to give His life as a ransom, so that sin's penalty might be paid. His face had been set toward Jerusalem for its accomplishment (Lk. 9:51). In His humanity, He shrank from it. In His deity, He must surely have been repelled by the realization that He must bear in His holy and sinless body the weight of sin's curse, and be forsaken by His Father, even if for three hours only. So He went off by Himself in the garden and cried out to the Father three times, "O my Father, if it be possible, let this cup pass from me; nevertheless, not as I will, but as thou wilt" (Mt. 26:39, 42, 44; cp. Mk. 14:36; Lk. 22:42).

What was the cup from which the Lord Jesus Christ sought deliverance? It was death—whether death in the garden through some mysterious assault from the devil (cp. Lk. 22:42–44; Heb. 5:7) or death on the cross (cp. Mt. 20:22; Jn. 18:11; see Mt. 26:39, *note*). In either case, the thing above all others that

Christ prayed for was not His own will but the Father's will. The Gethsemane prayer was a prayer of submission. The Son of God "humbled himself and became obedient unto death, even the death of the cross" (Phil. 2:8).

10. *The Crucifixion of Christ*

The crucifixion and resurrection of Christ form together the capstone of His earthly ministry. Had Christ not died, there could have been no resurrection. Had He not been raised, His death in the sinner's place would have been inconclusive.

Christ's crucifixion was not an afterthought with God but was determined before man's creation (Acts 2:23). All that took place before the cross pointed forward to it. All that has occurred since then focuses on it. Even in the eternal ages the wounds of Calvary will be visible in the hands and feet of the Saviour.

Christ's arrest and trial, and the attitudes and actions of His followers and the authorities who opposed Him, are important and should be studied carefully. Here, however, consideration is given only to the crucifixion (Mt. 27:33–51; Mk. 15:22–39; Lk. 23:33–49; Jn. 19:16–37).*

A. THE FACT OF THE CRUCIFIXION

That the crucifixion actually took place is beyond dispute. Not only the Bible, but contemporary secular historians as well, vouch for it.

Crucifixion was practiced by the Romans. When the cross was raised to a vertical position, the weight of the victim's body caused the nails to tear his hands and feet. His joints were wrenched and a great deal of blood drained from his veins. See *notes* at Ps. 22:7; Isa. 52:14.

This is the kind of bodily torture the Lord Jesus Christ suffered. To view His crucifixion simply as a fact of history is

---

*For the order of events following Christ's arrest, see Mt. 26:57, *note*, and at His crucifixion, Mt. 27:33, *note*.

inadequate. It is history indeed, but history with a personal impact—far more personal and filled with meaning than the assassination of a political leader, as moving as that may be. Christ's death was voluntary, vicarious, expiatory, and efficacious. See Lev. 4:3, *note*. He died for the ungodly (Rom. 5:6–8). On the cross He bore *our* sins in *His* body (1 Pet. 2:24). Christ's death was the most tragic death of history, for when He died a completely sinless victim was executed. At the same time His crucifixion is the basis of the best news mankind has ever had. Without the cross there can be no Gospel; for "Christ died for our sins, according to the scriptures" (1 Cor. 15:3).

B. The Meaning of the Crucifixion

The crucifixion was related to different personalities in different ways. Yet it has one central meaning for all: divine judgment of sin was justly met at the cross.

(1) Its Meaning in Relation to God the Father

In relation to God the Father, Christ's death meant that His righteousness in forgiving sinners was vindicated. In O.T. times, God pronounced and executed the sentence of the law against a sinner by means of a substitutionary animal sacrifice. At the cross He accomplished the same thing, but in an infinitely more efficacious way, through the sacrifice of His Son, "the Lamb of God," who served as the substitute for all men (Jn. 1:29; 1 Pet. 1:18–19; Rev. 5:6,12; 7:10; 13:8). See Lev. 16:5, *note*: Lev. 17:11, *note* 2. But there is a great difference. Although the O.T. sacrifices covered sins for the time being, until Christ should come, His sacrifice of Himself made full atonement for sin. See Lev. 16:6, *note*. And although the O.T. offerings had to be presented to God again and again, Christ's offering of Himself was once for all (Heb. 9:26, 28; 10:12,14). It need never be repeated.

So it was that, when Christ died, the veil of the temple was torn in two from the top to the bottom, opening the way into the immediate presence of God for every believer in His Son (Heb. 10:19–22). See *notes* at Mt. 27:51; Mk. 15:38.

(2) Its Meaning in Relation to God the Son

In relation to God the Son, the crucifixion meant that the work which He came to earth to do was accomplished. "It is finished!" He cried out just before He dismissed His spirit into the Father's care (Jn. 19:30; cp. Lk. 23:46). See Mt. 27:50, *note*.

Moreover, the crucifixion meant glorification for the Son. His prayer, "Father, the hour is come; glorify thy Son, that thy Son may also glorify thee" (Jn. 17:1), was answered. He had emptied Himself of that glory when He came into the world (Phil. 2:5–11; cp. Jn. 17:5). By the supreme act of His perfect obedience, the Son in turn glorified the Father.

Still further, Christ's crucifixion was the means of bringing many believers into glory (Heb. 2:10; cp. Isa. 53:11). In His high-priestly prayer He declared that the glory which His Father had given Him, He (Christ) had given to all who believe, "that they may be one, even as we are one" (Jn. 17:22).

(3) Its Meaning in Relation to God the Holy Spirit

In relation to God the Holy Spirit, the crucifixion attested the trustworthiness of the prophetic Word. "For the prophecy came not at any time by the will of man, but holy men of God spoke as they were moved by the Holy Spirit" (2 Pet. 1:21). See 2 Tim. 3:16, *note*; cp. *notes* at 1 Cor. 2:13; 2 Pet. 1:19.

About a thousand years before the crucifixion, David foretold some of Christ's words from the cross, "My God, my God, why hast thou forsaken me?" (Ps. 22:1; cp. Mt. 27:46; Mk. 15:34). A prediction that none of Christ's bones would be broken was made about the same time (Ps. 34:20; cp. Jn. 19:33, 36). That the Lord Jesus would be given vinegar to drink was also prophesied by the psalmist (Ps. 69:21; cp. Mt. 27:34; Jn. 19:29). Isaiah, seven centuries before Christ's death, said that the Suffering

111

Servant of God would be slain along with malefactors (Isa. 53:12; cp. Mt. 27:38; Mk. 15:27–28). See *notes* at Lk. 23:39, 43. Zechariah mentioned in the sixth century B.C. that Christ would be pierced (Zech. 12:10; cp. Jn. 19:34–37).*

(4) Its Meaning in Relation to Satan

In relation to Satan, the crucifixion of Christ meant that his defeat and doom were sealed. Since the time of his fall (Isa. 14:12–15), Satan has prosecuted relentlessly a warfare against the work of God. Satan's prime battle, from the time of man's creation, has been to destroy the seed of the woman, by which his own head is to be crushed (Gen. 3:15; Rom. 16:20). It was to break the Messianic line that the devil induced Herod to slay the infants at the time of Christ's birth (Mt. 2:16–18). It was to divert Christ from His path to the cross that Satan offered Him the kingdoms of this world, if He would fall down and worship him (Mt. 4:8–9). For Satan is the prince of this world, its god (Jn. 14:30; 16:11; 2 Cor. 4:4). See *notes* at Isa. 14:12; Rev. 13:8. But he was judged at Calvary, where Christ triumphed over him and all principalities and powers (Col. 2:15). So, although the execution of the devil's sentence is still future, he became fully aware that his judgment fell when the Victor became the victim of men's injustice and cruelty (Jn. 12:31). See Rev. 20:10, *note*; cp. *note* at Lk. 23:35.

(5) Its Meaning to Mankind

By His crucifixion, Christ paid the penalty for every sin ever committed by His people—those of the past and also those of the future. There is only one condition of forgiveness: faith in Jesus Christ as the Son of God and personal Saviour. To that part of mankind which rejects God's free offer of forgiveness and redemption, the crucifixion of Christ means little more than the death of a good man. But to those who believe on Him, His crucifixion

---

*For other examples of prophecies that were fulfilled when Christ was crucified, see Ch. II, p. 26f.

means everything. They can exclaim with Paul, "God forbid that I should glory, except in the cross of our Lord Jesus Christ, by whom the world is crucified unto me, and I unto the world" (Gal. 6:14).*

11. *The Resurrection of Christ*

All four Gospels speak of the bodily resurrection of Christ. It was not a spirit that walked the Emmaus Road with two of the Lord's disciples (Lk. 24:13–32). It was Christ Himself. The risen Christ told Thomas to look at His hands and touch His side (Jn. 20:27). Christ's resurrected body was a physical body— changed indeed, yet the same body that was crucified and buried.

It is no less an integral part of the Gospel "that he [Christ] rose again the third day according to the scriptures" (1 Cor. 15:4), than that He died. "And if Christ be not raised," says Paul, "your faith is vain; ye are yet in your sins" (v. 17).

A. THE FACT OF CHRIST'S RESURRECTION

Six contemporaries of Jesus Christ have asserted in Scripture the fact of Christ's resurrection: the four evangelists (Mt. 28:1–10; Mk. 16:1–14; Lk. 24:1–12; Jn. 20:1–18), and the apostles Paul and Peter (1 Cor. 15:1–20; 1 Pet. 1:3–5, 21).†

B. THE REASONS FOR CHRIST'S RESURRECTION

There are at least five reasons for Christ's resurrection: (1) because He is the Son of God, and it is not possible that He could be shackled by death (Acts 2:24); (2) to establish that His witness concerning Himself was true (Mt. 17:22–23); (3) to show that divine justice was satisfied by His death and, as a result, all that believe in Him are justified in the sight of God (Rom. 4:25);

---

*For a fuller discussion of Christ's death as it relates to mankind, see Ch. XII.

†For the order of events on the resurrection morning, see Mt. 28:1, *note* 4.

(4) to prove to mankind that Jesus Christ is the Son of God (Rom. 1:4); and (5) as a token to those who trust in Him, that they also will be raised (1 Cor. 15:20–23).

C. The Result of Christ's Resurrection

Christ is not a dead Saviour but a living Lord and Saviour. This is of inestimable value to all who have committed themselves to Him in faith. Because He lives, we shall live also (Jn. 14:19). A new life is imparted to us the day we place our trust in Him, life that is everlàsting (1 Pet. 1:3).

(1) Christ's Life Is the Believer's Life

Before He ascended into heaven the risen Christ said to His disciples, "I am with you always, even unto the end of the age" (Mt. 28:20). He is with His own people now. More than that, He is also *in* His own people now (Gal. 2:20; Col. 1:27; cp. Rom. 8:9). By His death He saves the believer from the penalty of sin and brings him to God (1 Pet. 3:18). By His life He saves the believer from the power of sin in daily living (Rom. 5:8–11).

(2) Christ's Resurrection Assures the Believer's Resurrection

Unbelievers as well as believers will be raised from physical death (Jn. 5:28–29). But there is a great difference in degree and in the time.

The resurrection of those who "have done evil" and have not received Christ as their Saviour will be unto condemnation. This resurrection will take place at the end of the millennium, when all the unregenerate will stand before the great white throne and then be cast into the lake of fire (Rev. 20:11–15).* Scripture reveals nothing concerning their resurrected bodies.

Those who "have done good" will be raised unto life (Rom. 8:11). To do "good" is to do the will of God. Jesus did good because He did God's will (Heb. 10:7). It is God's will, for

*See Ch. XV, p. 154.

example, that we should be obedient, worshipful, set apart to God and from the world system, and be thankful (Jn. 7:17; 9:31; Rom. 12:2; 1 Th. 4:3; 5:18; Heb. 13:21; 1 Pet. 2:15).

Paul says that the resurrected bodies of believers will be spiritual, incorruptible, and immortal (1 Cor. 15:42–44,51–53). They will be like Christ's resurrected body, that is, bodies of glory (Phil. 3:21; 1 Jn. 3:2). See 1 Cor. 15:52, *note*. The resurrection of Christ assures the believer in Him that he possesses His life today, and that his body will be redeemed and changed when the Lord Jesus comes to the air and takes His Church into His presence (Rom. 8:23; 1 Cor. 15:52; 1 Th. 4:16–17).*

12. *Christ's Ascension*

There are three accounts in the N.T. of Christ's ascension into heaven (Mk. 16:19; Lk. 24:50–51; Acts 1:1–9). The writer of the Hebrews epistle also alludes to it when he speaks of our great High Priest, "that is passed through the heavens" (Heb. 4:14, *lit.*).

After His resurrection Jesus was seen alive by a number of people, among them Mary Magdalene and other women, His eleven disciples on several occasions—some of them individually and at least twice collectively—and once by "above five hundred brethren" (1 Cor. 15:6). See Jn. 20:16, *note*.

Forty days after the resurrection (Acts 1:3) Christ led His disciples "as far as Bethany" which, from Jerusalem, is at the far side of the Mount of Olives (Lk. 24:50; cp. Acts 1:12). He instructed them to wait in Jerusalem for the Holy Spirit (Acts 1:4). They asked Him whether it was now the time when He would restore the kingdom to Israel. He replied that it was not for them to know but that it was in the Father's hands (vv. 6–7). He gave them His final command—to be witnesses concerning Him to the farthest part of the earth (v. 8). Then, while they were looking at Him, "he was taken up, and a cloud received him out of their

*See Ch. XV, p. 136ff.

sight" (v. 9). As they were still gazing into the sky, two men in white apparel spoke to them: "This same Jesus, who is taken up from you into heaven, shall so come in like manner as ye have seen him go into heaven" (v. 11).

Christ will come to the earth again visibly and bodily (Mt. 24:30; 25:31; Mk. 14:62; Rev. 1:7; 19:11–16). See Acts 1:11, *note*.

When the Lord Jesus ascended into heaven, the mission of His first coming, "to seek and to save that which was lost" (Lk. 19:10), was completed. He had accomplished His redemptive work but not His total work. At present He is acting on behalf of His mystical body, the Church. He intercedes for us, that we may be kept from sin (Rom. 8:32–34; Heb. 7:24–25). And, if we *should* sin, He is our Advocate, pleading our cause before the Father (1 Jn. 2:1–2). Meanwhile He is waiting—waiting for the time when He will catch up His own people in the rapture and until the Father sends Him back again to the earth to judge and to reign, when all His enemies will be put under His feet (Heb. 10:12–13).

CHAPTER XI

Sin

S IN is a universal fact of human life. Even a person who has never seen the Bible recognizes the difference between right and wrong. God's Word has a great deal to say about sin. Sin causes the spiritual death of the unregenerate and breaks the fellowship with God of those redeemed from its curse. Only the cross of Christ can reveal sin's enormity. Apart from Him and His payment of its penalty, the sinner has no hope.

1. *Sin Defined*

The English word "sin" in its various forms, and related words such as "trespass" and "transgression," appear more than 900 times in the Bible. Two major words in the original languages (Heb. *châtâ'*; Gk. *hamartía*), rendered "sin" in the English Bible, come from root verbs meaning *to err, to fail, to miss the mark*. In its biblical use sin may be defined as *that inherent attitude of mind which cause*s *men to be less righteous than God; that conduct which lacks conformity with the law and character of God*. Sin expresses itself in various ways—through self-will, pride, jealousy, bitterness, hatred, dishonesty, evil thoughts, immorality, lawlessness, and the like (Mk. 7:21–23; Gal. 5:19–21; cp. 2 Tim. 3:1–5). See Mk. 7:21, *note*.

The universality of sin is clearly declared in Scripture: "There is none righteous, no, not one. For all have sinned and come short of the glory of God" (Rom. 3:10, 23; cp. Gen. 6:5; Isa. 64:6). See Rom. 3:23, *note*.

2. *The Origin of Sin*

Sin began in the universe long before man's creation. It came with Satan's rebellion against God (Isa. 14:12–14, where see *note* at v. 12).

Sin was introduced into the human race when Satan induced Eve to eat the forbidden fruit, which Adam also ate (Gen. 3:1–6; cp. 1 Tim. 2:14). This was man's fall. See Gen. 3:6, *note*.

3. *The Effects of Sin*

Sin's entrance into the world brought with it certain results. (a) Sin separates man from God; for God is holy and cannot look with favor upon sin (Hab. 1:13; cp. 1 Jn. 1:5). After their transgression, Adam and Eve knew immediately that they were separated from God. That is why they hid themselves from Him (Gen. 3:8).

(b) When Adam fell, sin came upon all men. "By one man sin entered into the world, and death by sin, and so death passed upon all men, for all have sinned" (Rom. 5:12, where see *note*, p. 1217). Adam and Eve became sinners because they sinned. Since that time all men and women sin because they are sinners (Eph. 2:3). That is also their position before God. "The scripture hath concluded all under sin" (Gal. 3:22).

(c) "The wages of sin is death (Rom. 6:23)—death that is both spiritual and physical. See *notes* at Eph. 2:5; Heb. 9:27. "In Adam all die" (1 Cor. 15:22; cp. Ezek. 18:4, 20). Men love darkness rather than light because their deeds are evil. So condemnation must fall upon them in their sinful state (Jn. 3:19).

And (d) even creation fell under the curse of Adam's sin (Gen. 3:17–19; Rom. 8:19–22).

4. *The Remedy for Sin*

The remedy for sin is Christ. "For the wages of sin is death, *but* the gift of God is eternal life through Jesus Christ, our Lord"

(Rom. 6:23). "For as in Adam all die, *even so* in Christ shall all be made alive" (1 Cor. 15:22, where see *note*). On the cross Christ was made sin for us (2 Cor. 5:21). There He bore our sins in His body (1 Pet. 2:24).

Christ died for the ungodly (Rom. 5:6, 8). The unregenerate man is spiritually dead in sin. His condition does not result from sins committed daily but from his sinful nature. Christ died for him to redeem him. Unless he believes in and commits himself to the Saviour, he is lost forever and is the object of God's wrath (Jn. 3:36; Rom. 1:18; Eph. 5:6).

The believer in Christ is the recipient of new life in Him, spiritual life, everlasting life. See Jn. 3:36, *note*. The penalty for his sins was paid at Calvary. But what if he sins after he becomes a Christian? He need not sin, he does not wish to sin, in Christ he has power over sin. Yet despite all this, sometimes the believer sins. His position as a child of God is not changed, but his fellowship with God is broken. Again the remedy is Christ; for if the believer sins he has "an advocate with the Father, Jesus Christ the righteous; and he is the propitiation for our sins" (1 Jn. 2:1–2). Upon confession there is forgiveness and cleansing through the blood of Jesus Christ, and restoration of fellowship with the Father (1 Jn. 1:6–9). See Jn. 13:10, *note*.

CHAPTER XII

Salvation

SALVATION, as it relates to man's spiritual condition, is an act of God on behalf of man to absolve him from the guilt of sin and to deliver him from its penalty and liberate him from its power. It is God alone who saves; man cannot earn salvation by anything he does (Eph. 2:8–9). Salvation is freely offered to all who will receive it. Only one condition is required: faith on man's part—faith in Jesus Christ as the Son of God, who bore on the cross God's righteous judgment for sin and rose again to justify the believer (Jn. 5:24; Rom. 4:23–24; 10:9–10; 1 Cor. 15:1–4). See *notes* at Jn. 3:3,16.

Salvation begins with the individual when he commits himself to Christ as his Saviour (Acts 16:30–33; Rom. 10:8–13). Throughout his life on earth it continues, to enable him to reject sin's dominance day by day (Rom. 6:14; 8:2). It will be completed in the life to come, when the body as well as the soul, will be redeemed (Rom. 8:23; 1 Cor. 15:42–44; 1 Pet. 1:5). See Rom. 1:16, *note*.

Salvation has various aspects. Awareness of these, while not requisite for salvation, is an inducement toward fuller appreciation of God's grace and power to save. Some of these divine provisions are:

1. *Forgiveness*

Christ's payment of sin's penalty at Calvary involved forgiveness of sin (Eph. 4:32; 1 Jn. 2:12; cp. Mk. 2:5,7,10). To forgive sins is to remit them, that is, to separate them from the sinner. See Mt. 26:28, *note*. All the believer's sins, those of the past as well as those of the future, were atoned for by Christ's sacrifice

(Eph. 1:7; 1 Jn. 1:7). The believer must, however, confess the sins he commits after he becomes a child of God through faith (1 Jn. 1:9).

2. *Redemption*

On the cross Christ redeemed us. To redeem is to buy back that which at one time was owned but was lost. When our first parents sinned, they were disowned by God in a spiritual sense because of sin. They and all who have followed them were "sold under sin" (Rom. 7:14).

It is God's will that all mankind should be redeemed (2 Pet. 3:9). So He arranged to buy us back. The infinite price He paid was the death of His Son. For although our salvation is God's free gift to us, it cost God everything. Christ died for us, and when He did so, He purchased our salvation. Furthermore, He purchased *us* at the same time (1 Cor. 6:20; 7:23; Rev. 5:9; cp. 1 Cor. 3:23; 2 Cor. 8:9). See Rom. 3:24, *note*; cp. *note* at Ex. 6:6.

3. *Justification*

To justify is to declare righteous. Christ's death and resurrection effected the justification of the redeemed sinner (Rom. 4:25). Like salvation, justification is not earned by man but is received freely through faith in the blood of Christ (Rom. 3:24, 28; 5:1, 9; Gal. 3:24). See Rom. 3:28, *note*.

The believer's justification means that he is counted as righteous. God's own righteousness is imputed to him, just as man's sin was imputed to Christ (2 Cor. 5:21; cp. Rom. 4:22–24). See Jas. 2:23, *note*; cp. *notes* at Rom. 3:21; Phile. 18.

God is able to justify the sinner because His righteous demand that sin be penalized was met when Christ made atonement by shedding His blood. Expiation for sin was thus offered. See Rom. 3:25, *note*; cp. *note* at Lev. 16:6.

4. *Sanctification*

Sanctification and holiness are synonymous in Scripture. To sanctify means to set apart for God. In God's sight the believer in His Son is sanctified positionally the moment he commits himself to Christ (Heb. 10:10). In his practical experience the believer is sanctified by means of the Scripture (Jn. 17:17; Eph. 5:25-26). It is a part of the Holy Spirit's present ministry to apply the Word of God for progressive sanctification (Jn. 14:26).* Finally, the believer will be made like Christ when He appears the second time (1 Jn. 3:2-3). This is perfect sanctification. See Rev. 22:11, *note* 2; cp. *notes* at Zech. 8:3; Mt. 4:5.

5. *Glorification*

When Christ translates His Church to be with Himself,† God will give His people celestial bodies (1 Cor. 15:40, 49; Eph. 5:25-27; Col. 3:4). Christ has a glorious body (Lk. 9:31; cp. Mt. 17:2). When He appears we shall be like Him (1 Jn. 3:2). So our lowly bodies will be changed and fashioned like His glorious body (Phil. 3:21). This will be the final answer to His prayer, "The glory which thou hast given me I have given them, that they may be one as we are one" (Jn. 17:22). Already that glory is ours spiritually in our standing before God, as a part of our salvation. For "whom he called, them he also justified; and whom he justified, them he also glorified" (Rom. 8:30).

Forgiveness, redemption, justification, sanctification, and glorification are all a part of God's "so great salvation" in Christ.

*For a discussion of this subject, see Ch. XIII, p. 125.

†For a discussion of this subject, see Ch. XV, p. 136ff.

CHAPTER XIII

The Holy Spirit and the Church

I T has been pointed out that the Holy Spirit is one of the three
Persons of the Godhead, co-equal with the Father and the
Son.* The Spirit shares with the Father and the Son the same
attributes, glory, and power. At the same time, the Holy Spirit is
characterized by some properties and ministries peculiar to Him,
just as the Father and the Son operate in varied individual ways.

Trinity — 3 in unity

1. The Holy Spirit's Ministry Before Pentecost

In O.T. times and until the day of Pentecost, the Spirit acted
upon men to endue them with wisdom and power to execute
God's sovereign will. It was in this capacity that He inspired the
writing of the Scriptures, a work which continued until the New
Testament was completed. See Zech. 12:10, *note.*

During Christ's earthly ministry, He said that the Father
would give the Holy Spirit to those who asked for Him (Lk.
11:13). Shortly after Christ's resurrection He imparted the Spirit
to His eleven disciples as He "breathed on them" (Jn. 20:22).
These occasions were evidently preparatory to the later indwelling
and infilling of the Spirit at Pentecost, since just prior to His
ascension Christ told His followers to wait in Jerusalem until the
Holy Spirit came upon them (Lk. 24:49; Acts 1:4). See *notes* at
Lk. 11:13; Jn. 20:22.

2. The Holy Spirit's Ministry After Pentecost

On the day of Pentecost, Christ's disciples were baptized with
the Holy Spirit and filled in a special way (Acts 1:5, 8; 2:1-4).

*See Ch. III, p. 31ff.

The baptism with the Spirit initiated the N.T. Church, the mystical body of Christ, of which Christ is the Head (1 Cor. 12:13; Eph. 1:22–23; Col. 1:18).* See Heb. 12:23, *note*. This marked the beginning of the sixth dispensation, the Church age. See Acts 2:1, *note*.

Baptism with the Holy Spirit is requisite for membership in Christ's mystical body, the Church (Rom. 8:9,14–17). The Holy Spirit was first given to believers in a group—to Jews (primarily) at Pentecost, and to Gentiles in the house of Cornelius (Acts 10:24–48). See *notes* at Acts 2:4; 10:44. Every believer in Christ is born of the Spirit (Jn. 3:6), that is, born of God (Jn. 1:13; 1 Jn 5:1). Consequently all believers possess the Holy Spirit. It should be our goal to be filled with the Spirit (Eph. 5:18), an experience that comes only with complete submissiveness to Him.

The Holy Spirit's relation to the Church is important.

A. The Spirit Acts To Complete the Church

Christ said that when the Holy Spirit came He would convict the world of sin, of righteousness, and of judgment (Jn. 16:8). It is the Spirit's work to convince the unregenerate of their need of the Saviour and lead them to Christ by means of the Word (Rom. 10:17). Some will resist the Spirit's pleading, as Felix did when Paul spoke to him (Acts 24:24–25; cp. 7:51). Others will heed the Holy Spirit and be born anew, like the Ethiopian eunuch under Philip's preaching (Acts 8:26–39).

B. The Spirit Acts as a Helper

The Holy Spirit is the believer's Guide into all truth (Jn. 16:13), and his Comforter and Helper (Jn. 14:16). He intercedes with the Father on behalf of the believer, so as to guide him when he does not know how to pray (Rom. 8:26–27). See Jn. 14:16, *note*.

*The N.T. Church is seen in two forms: the mystical and invisible body of Christ, composed of all who are born again through faith in Him; and the local and visible church, which may contain some who only profess faith but are not truly saved.

124

C. The Spirit Bestows Gifts on the Church

Every believer in Christ is chosen to serve Him in bearing fruit (Jn. 15:16; Rom. 6:22; 7:4; Heb. 13:15). It is the Holy Spirit who bestows specific gifts to individuals. To some He imparts the gift of teaching; to others, the gift of faith (1 Cor. 12:4–11). The same Spirit gives His gifts to the Church as a whole, according to its needs (Eph. 4:8,11–16). Whatever the talent may be, the Spirit gives it (1 Cor. 4:7). Therefore a believer who holds a prominent place among his fellows is no better than he who has a seemingly lesser gift. Every gift is necessary to the whole body, to nourish it (Eph. 4:12–13). See *notes* at 1 Cor. 12:1; Eph. 4:11.

D. The Spirit Resolves Inner Conflict in the Believer

The believer in Christ possesses two natures: (1) the old sinful nature, which he inherited at birth; and (2) the new divine nature, which he received when he was born again. The old nature remains with him as long as he resides on earth. The new nature stays with him into the eternal ages beyond his physical death or his translation without dying.* During this life the believer experiences constant conflict between his old nature (referred to also as "the flesh") and his new nature. When the Christian yields to and follows the direction of the Spirit, he does not fulfill the desires of the flesh. If he lives according to the flesh, he will surely fail (Rom. 8:2, 4; Gal. 5:16–18). Resolution of his inner conflict is the work of the Holy Spirit. See *notes* at Rom. 6:6; 7:14,15; 1 Cor. 2:14; Eph. 4:24; Jude 23.

E. The Spirit Guarantees the Believer's Inheritance

The Holy Spirit pledges that the believer is secure in Christ. Even though the Christian may grieve the Spirit by committing sin, or quench Him through disobedience (Eph. 4:30; 1 Th. 5:19), the Holy Spirit keeps His seal upon him until the time when

*For discussion of this subject, see Ch. XV, p. 136ff.

his body is redeemed also (cp. Rom. 8:23 with Eph. 4:30). He who has begun a good work by baptizing a believer into the body of Christ will continue to carry on that work until the day of Jesus Christ (Phil. 1:6). The Holy Spirit is our earnest or promissory note, as it were (Gk. *arrabōn,* meaning *deposit, down payment, first installment, pledge*), so that we may have assurance of our security in Christ until He comes (2 Cor. 1:21–22; 5:5; Eph. 1:13–14). See *notes* at Eph. 1:13; Jude 1.

CHAPTER XIV

Christian Life and Service

THE Christian life is an entirely new life. Christ Himself lives in the believer (Gal. 2:20; Col. 1:27; cp. 2 Pet. 1:3–4). See Jn. 3:3, *note*. The unregenerate person cannot live the Christian life, for he does not have the life of Christ. Because God has redeemed us and given us new life in His Son, we ought to present ourselves to Him as a living sacrifice (Rom. 12:1–2).

1. *The Christian's Devotional Life*

Christian character will issue in devotion to God, conduct consistent with the heavenly calling, and good works. It finds expression in the fruit of the Holy Spirit: love, joy, peace, patience, gentleness, goodness, faith, humility, and self-control (Gal 5:22–23; cp. vv. 19–21). See Gal. 5:22, *note*. The Christian whose character is formed by the Spirit will also surely live under the control of the Spirit.

A. Worship

To worship God is to extol His Person and virtues, and to offer thanksgiving to Him for His mercies and grace, particularly for the gift of His Son, our Lord Jesus Christ. The English word "worship," which is used in both the Old Testament and the New Testament (Heb. *shâhâh*; Gk. *proskuneō*), means literally *to prostrate oneself*, that is, *to do reverence*.

Worship may be expressed externally by various means. In O.T. times, for example, the burning of incense in the tabernacle or temple was intended as an act of worship. Today, in the liturgy of the church, there are certain external forms that signify worship. It is not ritualism that is involved, but expressions of worship and praise—singing spiritual songs with feeling, reading and studying together God's Word, giving cheerfully for the Lord's work, and, of course, commemorating the Lord's Supper in accordance with His command. Obviously, external worship is valueless unless it is accompanied by an act of the heart.

Worship may also be rendered internally, the thoughts of the worshiper being lifted to God without any outward manifestation. Nor is it necessary to be in a church building to think of Christ's perfections and to offer praise and thanksgiving to God. Prayer is a part of worship. "Our Father, who art in heaven, *Hallowed be thy name*" (Mt. 6:9; cp. Jn. 17:1–5; Eph. 3:14–15). In the daily life of any individual he may grasp an opportunity to magnify the Lord (e.g. Phil. 4:20; Heb. 13:15).

The Psalms are filled with expressions of praise of God (e.g. Ps. 8; 19; 30; 47; 65; 84; 144; 150). In the last book of the Bible, worship is rendered to Christ, beginning with "Thou art worthy, O Lord, to receive glory and honor and power," and increasing in crescendo as the book unveils Christ's majesty (Rev. 4:11; 5:8–12; 7:12). Among the last words of Scripture are these: "Worship God" (Rev. 22:9).

An essential element of the new life in Christ is the spirit of worship. True worship is to love God and give Him reverence in our minds and hearts (Dt. 6:4–5, where see *notes*; Mt. 4:10; cp. Mk. 12:30), and to "worship him in spirit and in truth" (Jn. 4:24). Christian worship consists in ascribing divine perfections to God the Father, God the Son, and God the Holy Spirit and in adoring Him, not because one is rewarded for this adoration, but simply because God is God and worship is due Him.

B. KNOWLEDGE

When God created man He gave him a mind. God told Adam to subdue the earth and to have dominion over it, which certainly suggests that Adam was to learn and progress in knowledge. See

Gen. 1:28, *note* 2, p. 4. The capacity of the human mind is awesome. Think of man's genius to compose a symphony or explore space. These are God-given talents. Talents are distributed to be used. Far more important than knowledge of the arts and sciences, however, is knowledge of God. God has revealed Himself so that men may know Him—in the Bible, which is His written Word (Ps. 119:2–4, where see *note* 4 at v. 1), and through Jesus Christ, who is the living Word (Jn. 1:1–3, 14; 14:6–11; 17:26). See Jn. 1:18, *note.*

(1) Knowledge About God

Zophar asked Job, "Canst thou by searching find out God? Canst thou find out the Almighty unto perfection?" (Job 11:7). That there is a God, and that He acts in the universe, can be understood by all men, "for the invisible things of him from the creation of the world are clearly seen . . . even his eternal power and Godhead" (Rom. 1:20). However, knowledge about God is not limited to the evidences in nature concerning His existence. Infinitely more, in fact all we need to know about Him, is revealed in the Scriptures.

A person can learn much concerning God by reading the Bible, yet he may remain a lost soul, dead in trespasses and sins. More than knowledge *about* God is necessary, although the Christian should gather all the knowledge he can in this area. The most essential thing is to know God Himself; for, as Jesus said, "This is life eternal, that they might know thee, the only true God, and Jesus Christ, whom thou hast sent" (Jn. 17:3). One does not have the Christian life, and therefore cannot serve God acceptably, until He knows the Father and the Son.

(2) Knowing God

To know God Himself, then, is to know the Lord Jesus Christ, "who is the image of the invisible God . . . the express image of his person" (Col. 1:15; Heb. 1:3). Christ is made known in the Scriptures (Lk. 24:27, where see *note*; Jn. 5:39). Search the Scriptures, the O.T. as well as the N.T., and give thought to the things concerning Him. One of the ministries of the Holy Spirit is to give us understanding of the Bible. As you read it, ask Him to open your heart to receive the divine message. For the Spirit is our guide into *all* truth, brings *all* things to our remembrance, and shows us things to come (Jn. 14:26; 16:13).

The Christian should shun evil and walk in the light (1 Pet. 3:11; 1 Jn. 1:5–7; cp. Jn. 3:21). He should confess to God every known sin, and forsake it (1 Jn. 1:9; cp. 2:1–2). The devil will try in every way he knows to thwart God's children. He must be resisted with the armor that God provides (1 Pet. 5:8–9; cp. Eph. 4:27; 6:11–18; Jas. 4:7). Christ has already won the victory over Satan and the flesh (Col. 2:13–15; Heb. 2:14–15), and His strength is ours as we walk in the Holy Spirit (Gal. 5:24–26; Phil. 4:13). See 1 Jn. 1:7, *note*. A person who does not hear and obey God's Word can never know Him intimately (1 Jn. 2:3–5). These things are necessary for those who would live the Christian life.

C. Prayer

God speaks to us through His Word. We speak to Him through prayer. As the Bible offers daily spiritual food, so prayer provides daily spiritual breath. Prayer should not be neglected (Mt. 26:41; Lk. 18:1; 21:36; 1 Th. 5:17).

If prayer is to be heard and its petitions answered, certain attitudes are essential: (a) prayer must be offered in the name of the Lord Jesus Christ (Jn. 14:6, 13–14; 16:23, 26–27; cp. Heb. 10:19); (b) no sin should be harbored by the petitioner (Ps. 66:18); (c) prayer should be "in the Spirit" (Eph. 2:18; 6:18; Jude 20); and (d) prayer should be accompanied by faith and thanksgiving (Phil. 4:6; Col. 4:2; 1 Tim. 2:8; Jas. 1:5–6).

The model prayer which Christ taught His disciples (Mt. 6:9–13; Lk. 11:1–4) is more than a prayer to be memorized and recited publicly. It presents also a format that it is well to follow: to extol God, interest ourselves in His kingdom, petition Him about life's personal problems and needs, confess sin, and ask for His strengthening grace. See Lk. 11:2, *note*; cp. *notes* at

Mt. 6:9,12. In the Holy Spirit and with thanksgiving, the believer prays for these things and for all men (Eph. 6:18; 1 Tim. 2:1).

To learn about prayer it is helpful to read the prayers of some of God's servants of old, for example Elijah (1 Ki. 18:36–37), David (1 Chr. 29:10–19), Solomon (2 Chr. 6:12,14–42), Jeremiah (Jer. 32:16–23), Daniel (Dan 9:3–19), and Paul (Eph. 1:15–23; 3:14–21; Col. 1:9–11; cp. Phil. 1:3–4; Col. 1:3–4; 1 Th. 1:2–3).

Attitudes, instructions, forms, and examples of prayer are of little value unless they lead to the heart of the matter—personal prayer. The believer should set aside special times for prayer, allowing nothing to interfere. Jesus did this (Mk. 1:35; 6:46; Lk. 6:12). The Christian should live in an atmosphere of prayer, in which speaking with the Father in heaven is as normal as breathing. Christ lived in this way (Jn. 12:27–28). The child of God may talk with God in the assurance that he does not approach a throne of judgment but a throne of grace (Heb. 4:16). Consequently, because his entrance into the Father's presence is through the Son and in the Spirit, he can be bold in his praying, telling God everything in the confidence that He hears and answers the petitions of His children (Jn. 14:13–14; 15:7; 1 Jn. 5:14–15).

The same Holy Spirit who guides us into all Scripture truth, guides us also in our praying. That is what it means to pray "in the Spirit." Feeble men and women that we are, we need the Spirit's help. So it is that when we do not know how to pray or precisely what God's will may be, the Spirit Himself intercedes on our behalf according to the will of God (Rom. 8:26–27).

2. *The Christian's Personal Life*

Not only in his attitude toward God, but also toward himself and his fellow men, the believer offers himself in living sacrifice.

A. LOVE AND UNITY

The Christian life is a life of love and unity among believers. We who are Christ's have been made one in Him (Jn. 14:20; 27:20–23). By one Spirit we were baptized into one body (1 Cor. 12:12–13). As members one of another we ought to love each other (Jn. 15:12; 1 Jn. 3:11,14) and act in love (1 Cor. 12:31—13:13). See *notes* at 1 Cor. 12:31; 2 Jn. 5. Unity among believers is not something that requires organized regimentation. It springs from a bond of mutual love in the Holy Spirit, which already exists, but it needs to be guarded and nurtured (Eph. 4:1–6).

B. Christian Conduct

The N.T. constantly calls upon Christians to live according to the truth (Rom. 6:4; Gal. 5:16; Eph. 4:1; 5:8,15–17; Col. 1:10; 2:6–7; 1 Th. 2:10–12; 4:1,12; 2 Jn. 6). Our Lord said, "All things whatever ye would that men should do to you, do ye even so to them" (Mt. 7:12; cp. Eph. 4:32). Do not think that because Christ's Sermon on the Mount is His presentation of the principles of His earthly kingdom, it is not applicable for believers today. We are heirs of God's kingdom and should be governed by His laws, not as a means of salvation but as born-again subjects of the Lord Jesus Christ. See Mt. 5:2, 3, *notes*. "Whosoever transgresseth, and abideth not in the doctrine [teaching] of Christ, hath not God" (2 Jn. 9).

The Epistles give explicit instructions concerning the conduct of believers. A few Scripture references suffice to emphasize this: concerning business relationships (Rom. 12:11,17; Eph. 6:5–9), citizenship (Rom. 13:1–8, where see *note* at v. 4; cp. Mt. 22:21), family relationships (1 Cor. 7:1–16; Eph. 5:22—6:4, where see *notes*), morality (Rom. 13:12–13; 1 Cor. 6:18; Eph. 4:25–28; Col. 3:5–7), relationships among believers (1 Cor. 12:12–27; Gal. 6:1–10), social relationships (Rom. 12:18–21), speech (Eph. 4:29), stewardship (1 Cor. 16:1–2; 2 Cor. 8—9), temper (Eph. 4:30–32). "This is a faithful saying," says Paul, "and these things I will that thou affirm constantly, that they who have believed in God might be careful to maintain good works. These things are good and profitable unto men" (Ti. 3:8).

3. *The Christian's Service*

The Lord Jesus Christ was the Servant-Son (Isa. 42:1; 52:13; cp. Mk. 10:45). He was the perfect Servant, in whose steps we should follow (cp. 1 Pet. 2:21). He likened Himself to a vine and His followers to its branches (Jn. 15:1–15, where see *notes*). For fruitfulness in His service, therefore, the believer must abide in Him.

The Holy Spirit has given at least one gift to every believer (1 Cor. 12:4–11). The gifts are varied, so that each of us must evaluate his God-given talents, seek to know God's will about their use, and then serve Him with gladness and dedication.

A. WITNESSING

Christ commanded His apostles and all who would follow after them throughout this age to bear witness concerning Him to "the uttermost part of the earth" (Acts 1:8; cp. Mt. 28:18–20; Mk. 16:15; Lk. 24:44–48; Jn. 15:16). So then, the believer who does not tell others about the Saviour is disobedient to His command. Furthermore, compassion demands that the Christian testify for Christ. Had someone not carried the message to us, we might never have known Him (Rom. 10:13–15).

It is not possible for everyone to enter the ministry or go to a distant land to proclaim the good news of salvation in Christ. Nor does God expect everyone to do so personally. There are surely unsaved people near at hand—neighbors, associates in business, and acquaintances of other kinds—to whom we may speak about the Lord. And there are also ways of sharing in the proclamation of the Gospel at home and abroad. The Christ who died for you and me died for others too. It is the responsibility of every believer to reach out to them with the good news. This is a good work and will receive a reward (cp. Phil. 4:1; 1 Th. 2:19).

B. OTHER GOOD WORKS

The sinner is saved by God's grace through faith. Good works cannot earn him his salvation (Eph. 2:8–9). This is scriptural. But it is unscriptural not to remember, as the very next sentence in the Ephesian letter affirms, that the redeemed sinner has been "created in Christ Jesus unto good works" (v. 10), and that God expects him to do them. Good works on the part

133

of the believer are not simply a matter of choice; they are a Christian imperative.

Christ's life was filled with many good works (Jn. 10:32). The Holy Spirit began a good work when He regenerated believers in Christ (Phil. 1:6; cp. Jn. 3:5, 8). Eighteen times in the Epistles the expressions "good work" and "good works" are used relating to Christians (2 Cor. 9:8; Eph. 2:10; Col. 1:10; 2 Th. 2:17; 1 Tim. 2:10; 5:10, 25; 6:18; 2 Tim. 2:21; 3:17; Ti. 2:7,14; 3:1,8,14; Heb. 10:24; 13:21; 1 Pet. 2:12). James, although he does not employ the adjective "good," speaks fourteen times concerning works which, from the context, are obviously good works.

Some N.T. examples of good works are Mary's anointing of our Lord's head (Mt. 26:10), Dorcas' dressmaking for those who needed her help (Acts 9:36, 39), and certain acts of kindness performed by others (1 Tim. 5:10). The love of God in the heart is that which causes His people to have compassion on those in need and to help them (1 Jn. 3:16–18). James calls attention to the fact that a person who sees someone with virtually no clothing and without food, and does not come to his aid, has a dead faith (Jas. 2:14–17). Good works, then, are acts of love to those in physical, mental, and spiritual need, if those deeds are done in the name of the Lord Jesus Christ. So, too, are sacrificial giving (Heb. 13:16), efforts to promote righteousness on earth and retard evil (Rom. 12:21; cp. Mt. 5:13–16)—even the gift of a cup of water in Christ's name (Mk. 9:41).

All believers must stand before the judgment seat of Christ (Rom. 14:10; 2 Cor. 5:10), where our works as Christians will be tested. Some works will bring a reward to the workers; other works will cause the believers loss (1 Cor. 3:11–15, where see *note* at v. 14).

Throughout eternity God's servants will serve Him (Rev. 22:3). It is time to begin now. "Let your light so shine before men, that they may see your good works, and glorify your Father, who is in heaven" (Mt. 5:16).

CHAPTER XV

Things to Come

GOD has not left us in the dark about the future. He has given us in Scripture His over-all program as it relates to the earth, the heavens, and eternity. While He has not revealed all the details. He has made known much that we can understand. As a background for the study of future events, acquaintance with some of Daniel's prophecies is essential.

The Angel Gabriel told Daniel that a period of seventy weeks was coming, in which God would make reconciliation for the sins of Israel and bring in everlasting righteousness (Dan. 9:24–27). The seventy weeks (*lit.* seventy sevens) are weeks of years—a total of 490 years. These years are divided into segments (Dan. 9:25–27): seven weeks (forty-nine years), sixty-two weeks (434 years), and one week (seven years). The seventy weeks began with Artaxerxes' command to rebuild Jerusalem and its walls after Jerusalem's fall to Babylon. See Neh. 2:5, *note*. This was in 445 B.C. From that time until the crucifixion of Christ would be sixty-nine weeks (483 years). So sixty-nine weeks of Daniel's prophecy have been fulfilled. But the seventieth week (seven years) has not yet been fulfilled.

An intercalary period of history, after Christ's death and resurrection and the destruction of Jerusalem in A.D. 70, has intervened. This is the present age, the Church age. See Acts 2:1, *note*. During this time God has not been dealing with Israel nationally, for they have been blinded concerning God's mercy in Christ (Rom. 11, where see *notes* at vv. 1, 5, 17, 25, 26). However, God will again deal with Israel as a nation. This will be in Daniel's seventieth week, a seven-year period yet to come. See Dan. 9:24, *note*.

Some of Christ's Olivet Discourse relates to this prophetic week of years (Mt. 24:4-28), as does Revelation 6—19. It will be divided into two parts of three and a half years each—equivalent with the "beginning of sorrows" (Mt. 24:4-14, cp. v. 8) and the "great tribulation" (v. 21). "The prince that shall come," an evil person about whom more will be said later, will make a covenant with the Jews but will break it "in the midst of the week" (Dan. 9:26-27). There are four other Scripture references to a period of three and a half years in the same context: "a time and times and the dividing of time" (Dan. 7:25), "a time, and times, and half a time" (Rev. 12:14), 1260 days (Rev. 12:6), and forty-two months (Rev. 13:5). In each instance the allusion is to the latter half of Daniel's seventieth week, namely the "time of Jacob's trouble" (Jer. 30:7), the span described in Revelation 8:1—19:6. See Rev. 11:2, *note*.

In popular usage the whole period of Daniel's seventieth week has come to be known as the tribulation, though it is not so designated in Scripture. This is in contrast with the latter half of the week, which is called the great tribulation. The NSRB often uses "tribulation" to designate Daniel's seventieth week (see e.g. Rev. 7:14, *note*). So does this book. Hereinafter, when the word refers to the full seven-year prophetic period, it is placed within single quotation marks thus: 'tribulation.' Christ's term "great tribulation" always signifies the latter half of Daniel's seventieth week, not the full week.

The sequence of things to come does not begin with the 'tribulation,' however, but with the translation of the Church.

1. *The Rapture*

The rapture or translation of the Church is the next event in predictive prophecy. At a time not known precisely, the Lord Jesus Christ will descend from heaven and meet His Church in the air. When this occurs, all who have died in Christ will be raised and, together with a living generation of believers, will be translated into His presence, to be with Him forever (1 Th.

4:13-17; cp. 1 Cor. 15:51-57; also Jn. 14:3, where the rapture is intimated; 2 Th. 2:1). See 1 Cor. 15:52, *note*.

The day and hour when Christ will take His Church to be with Him is not made known in Scripture. There are, however, indications as to the temporal relation of the rapture to Daniel's seventieth week. Although not all Bible students agree about this,★ there are several intimations in the New Testament that the rapture will precede the 'tribulation' and that no part of the Church will pass through any portion of it.

(a) 1 Thessalonians 5:9: "God hath not appointed us [i.e. believers] to wrath, but to obtain salvation by our Lord Jesus Christ." The 'tribulation' will be a period when the wrath of God will fall upon the earth and those who dwell on it (Rev. 6:16-17; 11:18; 14:10,19; etc.). God's wrath comes upon unbelieving sinners, not on believers (Jn. 3:36). Judgment for sin will not be executed against those "who are in Christ Jesus" (Rom. 8:1; cp. Jn. 5:24). Christ bore divine wrath and judgment for us. The Church is in no way subject to these things (cp. Rev. 3:10).

(b) 2 Thessalonians 2:6-8. The Thessalonian Christians were concerned that the day of the Lord and of His wrath (Joel 2:1-2; Zeph. 1:14-18; see Joel 1:15, *note*) might already be present in their day. Paul assured them that the day of the Lord will not come until the man of sin is revealed (v. 3). Then he went on to say that the man of sin will not appear until the restrainer, or hinderer, is "taken out of the way" (vv. 6-8).

The man of sin, referred to also as "the son of perdition" (v. 3) and "that wicked one" (v. 8), is the "beast" of Revelation 13:1, concerning whom more will be said later. This person does not begin his activities until the 'tribulation' starts.

★Some Bible interpreters, called mid-tribulationists, hold that the rapture of the Church will take place halfway through the 'tribulation.' Others, called post-tribulationists, believe that the rapture will not occur until after the 'tribulation.' Still others, known as partial-rapturists, teach that only a select group, those who are waiting and watching for Christ, will be raptured. The position held by the editorial committee of the NSRB is that the rapture of the whole Church will take place *before* the 'tribulation,' i.e. the editors are pre-tribulationists.

Evidence suggests that the restrainer is the Holy Spirit, who is acting now through the Church to curb iniquity.* The Spirit resides within believers in Christ, who both collectively and individually are the Spirit's temple (1 Cor. 3:16; 6:19; cp. Rom. 8:9). The Holy Spirit is our seal until the day of redemption (Eph. 4:30; Phil. 1:6). Not until the Church is translated to heaven will He be "taken out of the way," resuming His ministry as it was before Pentecost.† Therefore the Church must be removed from the world before the 'tribulation' begins. See 2 Th. 2:3, *note*.

(c) Revelation 4:4. In his Patmos vision the Apostle John saw a door opened in heaven, and he was told, "Come up here, and I will show thee things which must be hereafter" (Rev. 4:1, where see *note*). John saw a throne, and surrounding the throne twenty-four elders clothed in white raiment, and wearing crowns of gold" (v. 4).

The identification of the elders should not be difficult. Since nowhere else in Scripture are celestial beings called elders, the elders of this passage are not likely to be angels, but rather men. Furthermore, nowhere in the Bible are angels pictured as wearing crowns. Elders, in both Old and New Testaments, are generally leading representatives of a company of people (e.g. Num. 11:16; Ti. 1:5, where see *note*). These twenty-four elders are said to be wearing crowns of gold. Their crowns (Gk. *stéphanoi*) are victors' wreaths, that is, they are rewards. Rewards are for the Church (Rev. 3:11; cp. 1 Cor. 3:9–16). They are associated with resurrection (Lk. 14:14). All these crowns will be awarded at one time, "in that day" (2 Tim. 4:8), which is the day of Christ, the day when He comes for His own. The twenty-four elders represent the Church rewarded, and this will be before the first seal of the 'tribulation' is broken (Rev. 6:1). See Rev. 4:4, *note*.

---

*Some expositors identify the restrainer as the visible church or civil government. The editorial committee of the NSRB believes the restrainer is a Person, the Holy Spirit.

†See Ch. XIII, p. 123.

The Church is not seen on earth after Daniel's seventieth week begins. In fact, the word "church" does not appear in Revelation from the beginning of the fourth chapter to the end of the book, at Revelation 22:16.

2. The Judgment Seat of Christ

"We must all appear before the judgment seat of Christ, that everyone may receive the things done in his body, according to that he hath done, whether it be good or bad" (2 Cor. 5:10). The statement applies to Christians (2 Cor. 1:1). Salvation is not involved here, for the judgment of our sins was met by Christ on the cross. This is a judgment of our deeds after we become Christians. See 2 Cor. 5:10, *note*.

The expression "judgment seat" is somewhat misleading. The Greek word (*bēma*) means a *tribunal, judicial bench, raised platform*, the kind of stand that might be used by an official when he judges an athletic contest and awards prizes. Details about the testing of the believers' deeds on earth are given in 1 Corinthians 3:11–15. Our works will be tested by fire. Some works will pass through the fire and will be purified in the process. Some deeds will be consumed by the fire, so that there will be nothing left. Only those works which survive the test will bring reward. Observe that it is not the size of any work that will count, but "of what *sort* it is" (1 Cor. 3:13). Notice also that none who stands before the tribunal will be lost. The loss will be of rewards. See 1 Cor. 3:14, *note*. There are different kinds of crowns for different kinds of service—crowns of life, of glory, etc. (1 Cor. 9:25; Phil. 4:1; 1 Th. 2:19; 2 Tim. 4:8; Jas. 1:12; 1 Pet. 5:4; Rev. 2:10).

2. The Marriage of the Lamb

At some time after the rapture of the Church, the marriage of the Lamb of God will take place (Rev. 19:7–9; cp. Jn. 1:36; Rev. 5:12; 6:1; 14:1). It will be on this occasion that the Lord

Jesus, the heavenly Bridegroom, will be united with the Church, His bride, in accordance with God's purpose for them, and they will be one indeed (Rom. 7:4; 2 Cor. 11:2; Eph. 5:25–27, 32; cp. Mt. 25:10; Jn. 3:29; Rev. 21:1–2, 9–10; 22:17). See *notes* at Rev. 19:7, 8.

4. The 'Tribulation'

Daniel's seventieth week will be a period during which judgments will fall upon people everywhere on earth. Israel will suffer unprecedented trouble during its latter half. Gentile world power will be destroyed under climactic divine judgment. The 'tribulation' is a part of the day of the Lord, mentioned in both the O.T. and the N.T., and which extends over a much longer period than seven years. In the day of the Lord, God will intervene in the world's affairs in dramatic ways—sometimes in blessing, sometimes in judgment. See Rev. 19:19, *note*; also *notes* at Isa. 10:20; Joel 1:15; Zeph. 1:7.

The day of the Lord should not be confused with the day of Christ, although in a sense there is a link between the latter and the former. The day of Christ is exclusively a N.T. expression. It is for the Church only and relates to divine favor and rewards at the time of the rapture. See 1 Cor. 1:8, *note*. The day of Christ is the first event of blessing in the day of the Lord; the 'tribulation' is the first event of judgment in the day of the Lord.

A. The Great Tribulation Predicted

Prophecies concerning the latter half of Daniel's seventieth week were made centuries before Christ mentioned it to His disciples. Moses said that a time of trial would come "in the latter days," during which Israel would turn to the Lord (Dt. 4:27–30). Jeremiah predicted its coming, calling it "the time of Jacob's trouble" (Jer. 30:1–3, 7–11; see notes at vv. 7,11). Daniel alluded to the great tribulation as "a time of trouble, such as never was since there was a nation even to that same time"

(Dan. 12:1). In Christ's Olivet Discourse (Mt. 24—25), He predicted a time of "great tribulation, such as was not since the beginning of the world to this time, no, nor ever shall be" (Mt. 24:21). Paul spoke of the great tribulation too (2 Th. 2:1–12).

B. THE NATURE AND PURPOSE OF THE 'TRIBULATION'

As has already been pointed out, the 'tribulation' will be an era of divine wrath upon the earth (Rev. 6:16–17; 11:18; 14:7, 10,19; 15:4,7; 16:1,7,19; 19:1–2). Sometimes God will employ wicked instruments to accomplish His judgments. He will, for example, allow the dragon (i.e. the devil) to persecute Israel (Rev. 12:3,12–17). Satan also will use his own agents, for instance the beast out of the sea, to blaspheme God and wage war with the 'tribulation' saints (Rev. 13:5–8).

One of the divine purposes of these judgments is to prepare Israel to recognize the Lord Jesus Christ as their Messiah, so that they will turn to Him. Another reason for God's wrath is to judge the nations for their lawlessness and rebellion against Him.

C. PRINCIPAL ACTORS IN THE 'TRIBULATION'

The actors in the 'tribulation' are composed of supernatural beings, human beings, and symbolic figures.

(1) The Lord Jesus Christ, the central figure of all revelation, identified here as a Lion (Rev. 5:5), a Lamb (Rev. 5:8,12,13; 6:1; 7:10, 17; 12:11; 14:1, 4, 10; 17:14; 19:7,9), a mighty angel (Rev. 10:1–3), The Word of God (Rev. 19:13), and King of kings and Lord of lords (Rev. 19:16). In the 'tribulation' He will act in judgment against Israel and the nations, for the 'tribulation' is said to be "the wrath of the Lamb" (Rev. 6:16–17). It is the ascended Christ who will break open the seals of the seven-sealed scroll of judgments (Rev. 6:1—8:1). It is the same Person, the Lamb, who will seal 144,000 Jews (Rev. 7:1–8). The kingdom of this world will be delivered to Him (Rev. 11:15). It is He who will destroy His enemies when He comes in power and glory (Rev. 19:11–16).

(2) Satan, identified also as that ancient serpent, the devil (Rev. 12:9,12,15,17), the dragon (Rev. 12:3, 4, 7, 9, etc.; 13:2, 4; 16:13), the accuser of the brethren (Rev. 12:10). Satan is the one who will turn against Israel to persecute her relentlessly (Rev. 12:13) and who will energize the beast to break his treaty with the Jews and to blaspheme Almighty God (Rev. 13:1-9; cp. Dan. 7:24-25; Mt. 24:15).

(3) Michael, elsewhere identified as the archangel (Jude 9), and "the great prince who standeth for thy [Daniel's] people," Israel (Dan. 12:1). Michael will cast Satan out of the heavens and to the earth when the devil is venting his hatred on Israel (Rev. 12:7-12).

(4) The two witnesses (Rev. 11:3-12). These servants of God will have power similar to that of Moses and Elijah (Rev. 11:6; cp. Ex. 7:19; 1 Ki. 17:1; 18:1; Jas. 5:17). They will bear testimony to the Lord Jesus until they are slain by the beast. Their dead bodies will lie in Jerusalem's streets for three and a half days. Then God will raise and translate them to heaven while their enemies view their ascension.

(5) The woman clothed with the sun (Rev. 12:1-6). The context makes it clear that she represents Israel, out of whom Messiah came (cp. Rom. 9:5). The dragon will marshal every power at his command to devour her, but God will guard her among the nations for 1260 days, the latter half of the 'tribulation.'

(6) The beast out of the sea (Rev. 13:1-10; 17:8-17; cp. 11:7). Scripture has a great deal to say about this person. It is highly important to read Daniel 2, 7, and 9, and to consult all the *notes* in these three chapters, in addition to the passages concerning him in Revelation and elsewhere.

Nebuchadnezzar, king of Babylon, had a dream concerning an image of a man. Daniel interpreted the dream, telling the king that the image represented four world empires. Nebuchadnezzar was the image's head of gold; thus the first empire was Babylon. Succeeding kingdoms, represented by other parts of the image, were to be Medo-Persia, Greece, and Rome. See Daniel 2, with all *notes*. In this dream the kingdoms are described from man's viewpoint—as a human figure. Later, when Belshazzar reigned in Babylon, Daniel himself had a dream, in which the empires appear as viewed by God—as beasts. See Daniel 7, with all *notes*.

Babylon, Medo-Persia, and Greece fell in succession. Then came Rome, which was the dominant power in the world at the time of Christ. Under Rome's authority Christ was crucified and Jerusalem fell. Although the empire was later divided into eastern and western parts, symbolized by the two legs of Nebuchadnezzar's image, it never became a ten-kingdom alliance, as suggested by the ten toes of the image (Dan. 2:42) and the ten horns of the fourth beast (Dan. 7:7). Nebuchadnezzar's image, Daniel said, would be destroyed by "a stone cut without hands" (Dan. 2:34–35, 44–45). This stone was a prophetic picture of Christ (cp. Ex. 17:6; 1 Cor. 10:4; 1 Pet. 2:3–8), whose kingdom will never be destroyed (Dan. 2:44–45). The fourth beast of Daniel's dream, like its counterpart in the image of Nebuchadnezzar's dream, will be destroyed by the Lord at His coming (Dan. 7:22, 26–27). See Rev. 17:12, *note*.

The beast of Revelation 13:1–10 will be the head of the predicted ten-kingdom power frequently referred to as the revived Roman Empire. He is said to have ten horns and ten crowns (Rev. 13:1) and to be a composite of the beasts of Daniel 7. He is identical with the "little horn" (Dan. 7:8), "the prince that shall come" (Dan. 9:26), "that man of sin . . . the son of perdition . . . that wicked one" whom the Lord will "destroy with the brightness of his coming" (2 Th. 2:3–4, 8). See *notes* at Rev. 13:1, 2, 3; 19:20.

At the beginning of Daniel's seventieth week, this beast will come before the world as a political messiah. His ten-kingdom federation will evidently be formed almost exclusively by treaty rather than by military conquest (Rev. 17:17; cp. 6:2). It is at this time that he will make a seven-year covenant with the Jews, which he will later break (Dan. 9:27). He will exalt himself above God (Dan. 7:25; 2 Th. 2:4) and "cause the sacrifice and oblation to cease, and for the overspreading of abominations he shall make desolate" (Dan. 9:27; cp. Mt. 24:15). At the same time

Israel will experience "great tribulation, such as was not since the beginning of the world to this time, no, nor ever shall be" (Mt. 24:21).

(7) The beast out of the earth (Rev. 13:11–17). Whereas the first beast will be a political ruler, the second beast will be a religious leader who will take to the first beast the worship of all who dwell on the earth (v. 12). Though he has two horns *like* a lamb, this false prophet speaks like a dragon. He will be the principal figure of the apostate church, which will be attached and subservient to the political ruler. See Rev. 13:11, *note*.

(8) The woman arrayed in purple and scarlet (Rev. 17:1–7,18). This "great harlot that sitteth on many waters" is the apostate religious system of the 'tribulation.' Her sway will include all Christendom, for she is said to sit upon a scarlet-colored beast, the beast of Revelation 13:1. In whatever place his ten-kingdom empire rules, she too will be there. These loathsome figures represent, therefore, political Babylon and religious Babylon. Just as the dragon turns against Israel, that is, the woman clothed with the sun (Rev. 12:1–6), so also the beast betrays the apostate church, that is, the woman arrayed in purple and scarlet (Rev. 17:15–16). Both Babylons are doomed under divine judgment (Rev. 18). See Rev. 18:2, *note*.

D. Armies of the 'Tribulation'

Seven armies will be prominent during Daniel's seventieth week. Three are heavenly and four earthly.

(1) Michael's army (Rev. 12:7–10). Midway through the 'tribulation' Michael's angelic army will cast Satan and his army out of heaven.

(2) The dragon's army (Rev. 12:7). The only battle in which this army engages during the 'tribulation' is that with Michael and his angels. After the millennium, Satan will gather other armies to wage war against the saints of God (Rev. 20:7–9).

(3) The army of the beast, which may be termed the army of the restored Roman Empire (Rev. 16:13–16; 19:17–19). This army, in defending Palestine for the beast, not for the Jews, will go to Armageddon to do battle with the kings of the north, the

south, and the east. The beast and his forces will be destroyed there at the coming of Christ. See Rev. 19:17, *note*; cp. *note* at 16:16.

(4) The army of the king of the south (Dan. 11:40). It appears that this king and his army will be allied with a ruler from the north. The king of the south will come up from Africa and attempt to enter Palestine through Egypt. He too will be destroyed.

(5) The army of Gog and Magog, or the king of the north (Ezek. 38:1–6; cp. Zech. 12:1–9; 14:1–3). This points to a future Russian army. (The Gog and Magog of Ezekiel 38 are not to be confused with the Gog and Magog of Revelation 20:8, who do not appear until after the millennium.) A confederation of nations, headed up by Russia, will go down to Palestine to take the land (Dan. 11:40). It will be destroyed by the Lord. See Ezek. 38:2, *note*; cp. *notes* at Zech. 12:1; 14:4.

(6) The armies of the kings of the east (Rev. 16:12; cp. Dan. 11:44). These forces, probably from the Far East, are independent of the armies of the northern and southern alliance. God will draw armies from the distant corners of the earth to Palestine, so that He may destroy them (Zech. 12:2–3, 9).

(7) The army of the King of kings and Lord of lords (Rev. 19:11–16). The great tribulation comes to its conclusion with the second advent of Christ, who will descend with His armies. He alone will smite the nations and destroy them. Thus He will bring to its end "the times of the Gentiles" (Lk. 21:24), which began when Judah was taken captive by Babylon (2 Chr. 36:6–7). See Rev. 16:19, *note*; also *note* at Lk. 21:24. With Christ's coming, the beast and the false prophet will be cast into the lake of fire, and Satan will be bound for 1000 years (Rev. 19:17—20:3).

E. A Panoramic View of Daniel's Seventieth Week

Christ's Olivet Discourse is mentioned in all the Synoptic Gospels. In these three records the 'tribulation' is presented in Matthew 24:4–28, Mark 13:5–23, and Luke 21:8–11, 25–28. Matthew's account is the best known and easiest to follow. But because it is highly condensed, it does not give the colorful details of Revelation 6—19.

The 'tribulation' begins with the breaking of the first seal of the seven-sealed scroll (Rev. 6:1). The first horseman rides forth "conquering, and to conquer" (Rev. 6:2, where see *note*), followed by three other horsemen (vv. 3–8). The inflictions that these riders bring upon the earth—a false messiah, wars and rumors of wars, famines, pestilences, and death—are parallel with the events in our Lord's prediction concerning the early part of the 'tribulation' (Mt. 24:4–8). In the beginning of sorrows, judgment upon judgment will fall on the earth. They will come in three series of sevens: first, the breaking of seven seals in sequence (Rev. 6:1—8:1). When the seventh seal is broken, seven trumpets begin to sound, one after another (Rev. 8:2—11:18). The trumpet blasts are followed by the pouring out in rapid succession of the judicial contents of seven bowls or vials of wrath (Rev. 16:1–21). Parenthetic passages occasionally interrupt the flow of the narrative (e.g. Rev. 7:1–17; 10:1—11:18; 12:1—14:20).

While these judgments are coming, the Gospel of the kingdom will be proclaimed in all the world (Mt. 24:9–14). See Rev. 14:6, *note*. People will be saved. One hundred and forty-four thousand Jewish people will be sealed by God as His servants (Rev. 7:4–8). A "great multitude . . . of all nations, and kindreds, and peoples, and tongues" who confess allegiance to the Lamb will be saved (Rev. 7:9–17, where see *note* at v. 14).

In summation, the false messiah, the beast who heads the ten-kingdom power of the last days, makes his covenant with Israel. Catastrophic divine judgments begin to plague all that dwell on earth, and the earth itself. The political climate is one of unrest. The beast then breaks his covenant (Dan. 7:27; Mt. 24:15). Israel suffers under the beast the greatest persecution of all the ages (Mt. 24:15–26, where see *note* at v. 16). This is during the latter half of Daniel's seventieth week, the great tribulation. The nations array themselves to battle against the beast, not because they intended to come to the aid of Israel but because they are angered by the beast and also because they covet the wealth of the Holy Land—possibly its oil and mineral deposits. It is at this time that the ascended Christ arises from His Father's right hand and comes to earth in power to destroy His enemies and put them under His feet (Mt. 24:27–28; cp. Ps. 110:1; Mt. 22:44; Acts 2:35; Heb. 1:13; 10:12–13). What begins with a false messiah riding a white horse on earth, ends with Christ the Lord descending on a white horse from heaven to earth as the Faithful and True, the Word of God, King of kings and Lord of lords. See Mt. 24:3, *note*.

5. The Second Coming of Christ

The Lord Jesus Christ will return visibly and bodily to the earth. At His ascension two men in white said to the apostles, "Ye men of Galilee, why stand ye gazing up into heaven? This same Jesus, who is taken up from you into heaven, shall so come in like manner as ye have seen him go into heaven" (Acts 1:11). The Lord Jesus was seen when He ascended bodily to heaven. The same Jesus will be seen when He descends bodily from heaven. He will come in power and great glory (Mt. 25:31; Rev. 19:11–16).

A. CHRIST'S RETURN PREDICTED IN SCRIPTURE

Although expressions such as "the return of Christ" and "the Lord's second coming" are not used in the Bible, the Lord's majestic second advent is predicted in both the O.T. and the N.T. The prophets did not always distinguish between His first and second advents, between His coming to earth in humiliation and His coming in majesty (1 Pet. 1:10–11). Sometimes they spoke of both advents at the same time (e.g. Ps. 22; Isa. 9:6–7; 61:1–2, where see note at v. 2; Zech. 9:9–10). But when they prophesied concerning His coming to reign on an everlasting throne, and said that He would judge His enemies, that the earth would be filled with the knowledge of the Lord and all nations would turn to Israel for blessing, they were speaking of what we now call the second coming of Christ. None of these things occurred during His first advent. They must come to pass, or the Word of God is not trustworthy. For examples of O.T. prophecies about the Lord's coming in power to reign on an everlasting throne in righteousness and peace, see 2 Sam. 7:16; Ps. 2:8–9; Isa. 2:2–4; 11:9–10; 32:1,18; Jer. 3:17–18; Dan. 2:44; Mic. 4:2–5; Zeph. 3:14–17; Zech. 12:6–9; 14:9.

In His last-recorded words the Lord Jesus promised He would come again (Rev. 22:20). Earlier He said He would return in power (Mt. 24:27; 25:31). The promise made at His ascension has already been mentioned (Acts 1:11). The Epistles allude to His return also (Col. 3:4; 1 Th. 1:10; 2:19; 3:13; 2 Th. 2:1, 8; Ti. 2:13; 2 Pet. 1:16; 1 Jn. 3:2; Jude 14), as does the Apocalypse (Rev. 1:7–8; 19:11–16; 22:12, 20). See 1 Cor. 1:7, *note*.

B. THE TIME OF CHRIST'S RETURN

It is impossible to know precisely the day or the hour when the Lord will return to the earth (Mt. 24:36; 25:13). Scripture gives no warrant to attempt to do so. When the apostles asked the Lord Jesus, after His resurrection, "Lord, wilt thou at this time restore again the kingdom to Israel?" He replied, "It is not for you to know the times or the seasons, which the Father hath put in his own power" (Acts 1:6–7, where see *note* at v. 6).

It is feasible, however, to relate the time of the Lord's return to earth, to the 'tribulation' and the millennium. The event will immediately follow the great tribulation (Mt. 24:29–30). It will immediately precede the millennium (Mt. 25:31–32).

The millennium is the period of Christ's earthly reign. Since there can hardly be a kingdom without a king, it seems obvious that the Lord will return before the millennium.*

*This view is what is known as premillennialism, the interpretation held by the editors of the NSRB. There are two other conceptions. (1) Amillennialism, a word which denotes that there will be no millennium (the prefix *a* meaning *without*). Some amillennialists, but certainly not all of them, look for the imminent return of Christ. They hold that the promises made to Israel apply to the Church, and that the predictions concerning His earthly reign must be spiritualized or have their fulfillment in eternity. (2) Postmillennialists (*post* means *after*) propose that through the preaching of the Gospel the world will get progressively better. Some of them postpone the kingdom for at least 1000 years. Others suggest that the kingdom reign of Christ is now, between His first and second advents while He is seated at the right hand of the Father.

C. The Manner of Christ's Return

The Lord's second coming will be a spectacular event. Nature will announce it—the sun and moon will be darkened, stars will fall from heaven, and the powers of the heavens will be shaken. There will be some sort of sign in the sky (perhaps the glory of Christ Himself) when He returns "in the clouds of heaven with power and great glory" (Mt. 24:29-31). He will descend to the Mount of Olives, and an earthquake will rend the mountain (Zech. 14:4, where see *note*). Every eye will see Him (Rev. 1:7).

The Lord Jesus will not be alone when He comes again. "Behold, the Lord cometh with ten thousands of his saints" (Jude 14; cp. Zech. 14:5; 1 Th. 3:13). All the holy angels will accompany Him (Mt. 25:31), and the armies of heaven will also follow Him (Rev. 19:14).

D. The Purpose of Christ's Return

Christ will come back to the earth to accomplish God's sovereign will in respect to the overthrow of His enemies, the conversion and restoration of Israel, and the establishment of justice and peace on the earth. The Lord's return will bring to pass unfulfilled prophecies concerning the setting up of the kingdom of David's greater Son. See Acts 1:11, *note*.

6. *Four Judicial Acts*

All divine judgment has been committed to God the Son (Jn. 5:22; Acts 17:31). See Rev. 19:11, *note* 3. When Christ returns He will act speedily, sternly, and righteously, inflicting punitive judgment upon some and rendering gracious justice and deliverance to others.

A. Beast and False Prophet Judged

When the Lord and His armies destroy the armies of the beast, Christ will promptly consign the beast and the false prophet to the lake of fire (Rev. 19:20).

149

B. Satan Imprisoned

At virtually the same time that the beast and the false prophet meet their doom, the devil will be bound with a chain, cast into the abyss, and sealed there for 1000 years (Rev. 20:1–3). After the millennium, Satan will be cast into the lake of fire along with death and hell, but he is not there yet. At the end of the millennium, he will be loosed for a time. He will go out to deceive the nations in his final rebellion. Then he will be cast into the lake of fire, where he will remain forever (Rev. 20:7–10). See *notes* at Lk. 16:23; Rev. 20:10.

C. Judgment of the Gentiles

When the triumphant Lord has executed judgment against the dragon and the two beasts, He will sit upon His glorious throne on earth. Among His first official acts as King will be His judgment of the Gentiles. He will place the sheep, composed of those Gentiles who have been saved during the 'tribulation,' on His right hand. On His left hand He will assemble the goats, composed of all the Gentiles who have rejected Him during the same period (Mt. 25:31–46).

Do not be misled into supposing that various nations will be separated, each as an entire national body. This judgment, like others, has to do with individuals. Individual Gentiles out of all the nations will be designated either as belonging with the sheep or with the goats.

The test of this judgment will be how individual Gentiles treated Christ's brethren—whether brethren according to the flesh (i.e. Jews) or brethren according to the Spirit (i.e. saved people)—during the 'tribulation.' None of the Gentiles will be saved by his works, although kindness to Christ's brethren, which will be at great personal risk (Rev. 13:15–17), will certainly be a good work. Such kindness will be a proof of faith in Christ. It is by faith in Him alone that salvation is offered.

In this judgment, then, Gentile believers are the sheep. Unconverted Gentiles are the goats. The sheep will be left on earth to enter the millennium. The goats will be cast "into everlasting fire, prepared for the devil and his angels" (Mt. 25:41). See Mt. 25:32, *note*.

D. JUDGMENT OF ISRAEL

Israel will also be judged when Christ ascends His throne of glory. Again the judgment will not be of the nation as a unit, but of individual Jews (Ezek. 20:33–38; Mal. 3:2–5). The nation will have been brought back to the land of Palestine (Dt. 30:1–10; Isa. 11:11–16; 49:22–23; 60:9–10; Jer. 16:14–15; 23:3, 7–8; 30:3; 33:7–9). See Dt. 30:3, *note*. The rebels among them will be purged. Those who have turned to the Lord, after recognizing at last that He whom they pierced is indeed their Messiah (Rev. 1:7; cp. Zech. 12:10), will enter millennial blessing. See Ezek. 20:37, *note*.

7. *The Millennium*

The millennium is the period of 1000 years (see Rev. 20:2, *note*) when Christ will reign over the earth as King. His blood-purchased people of all the ages will rule with Him, including those who have been slain during the 'tribulation.' The latter will have been raised at His coming, as the final segment of the first resurrection (Rev. 20:5–6, where see *note* at v. 5).

The word "millennium" is mentioned six times in Revelation 20:2–7. It is from this passage that Christ's earthly reign gets its name—the millennium.

The millennium is the last of the economies or dispensations* which condition human life on earth. It is the Kingdom age. See Kingdom, Rev. 20:4, *note*. Few subjects, if any, occupy as much space in Scripture as the millennial kingdom.†

*See Ch. VII, p. 53f.

†See Ch. X, p. 98.

A. Government During The Millenium

The government of all the earth will be under direct theocratic rule, with Christ as its universal King (Dan. 7:13–14, 27; Mic. 4:3; cp. Zech. 9:10). The moral characteristics of the kingdom will be righteousness and peace (Isa. 2:4; 9:6–7; 33:5; Hos. 2:18). Justice will prevail for everyone (Isa. 11:5; 42:1, 4; Jer. 23:5). Truth will be the basis of all government (Isa. 16:5; 42:3; Jer. 33:6; Zech. 8:3).

B. Subjects of the King

No unregenerate people, Jews or Gentiles, will enter the millennium (Mal. 4:1; Mt. 25:41, 46; cp. Isa. 1:19–20; Jer. 30:23–24; Mic. 5:15). Only those who have faith in Christ, either Jews or Gentiles, will inherit the kingdom (Jer. 30:18–22; Mal. 4:2; Mt. 25:34). It might be supposed, therefore, that in such an ideal situation—with a perfect Ruler whose subjects are composed of believers only, and with Satan banished and the Holy Spirit active—sin and rebellion would have no place. Time will prove that this is not so. When the millennium is over, God will have taken mankind around a full cycle of tests in respect to obedience to Him. In every circumstance thus far in history man has been a failure. He fell short of the mark in his innocence, he fell short when he was aware of his moral responsibility, he fell short when he governed himself, he fell short as a recipient of unconditional promises, again under the law he fell short, and today, in an age when divine grace is especially prominent through Christ, he continues to fall short. He will fail once more under Christ's personal reign of truth and justice. See Gen. 1:28 (heading), *note* 3.

C. Worship During the Millennium

Worship of the one true God will be universal at the beginning of the millennium (Zeph. 3:9; Zech. 14:16; Mal. 1:11). Worship will be according to knowledge (Isa. 11:9; Hab. 2:14, where see *note*; Zech. 8:20–23, where see *note* at v. 23; cp. Isa. 41:20;

52:6–10; 54:13). It will be under the control of the Holy Spirit (Isa. 59:21; Ezek. 36:26–28; 37:14; Joel 2:28–29).

There will be a temple on a high mountain in Jerusalem, to which all nations will go to offer praise to God (Ezek. 40:1–4; 41:1; cp. Ezek. 37:27–28). See Ezek. 40:5, *note*. An altar will stand in the temple (Ezek. 41:22), a place of communion with God. Sacrifices will be offered to Him (Ezek. 43:18–27, where see *note* at v. 19). Christ's sacrifice of Himself, which superseded the offerings of the Aaronic priesthood (Heb. 7:1—8:5), was an offering made once for all (Heb. 10:9–18). Therefore, the sacrifices of the millennial temple will be made, not as offerings for sin but as a memorial of Him just as in the Church age the bread and the wine of the Lord's table are in remembrance of Christ's death on our behalf (1 Cor. 11:23–26).

D. General Conditions on Earth During the Millennium

Those who enter the millennial kingdom (regenerate people only) will be normal human beings. They will marry and reproduce, and most of them will die (Jer. 30:18–20; Ezek. 47:22; cp. Jer. 31:29). Nevertheless, life beyond "threescore years and ten" will be the norm rather than the exception (Isa. 65:18–20; cp. Ps. 90:10). There will be work to do (Isa. 62:8–9; 65:21–23) and pleasures to enjoy (Isa. 9:3–4; 25:8; 66:10–13). The fruits of the fields will flourish (Isa. 30:23–24; 35:1–2), prosperity will increase (Isa. 65:21–23; Jer. 31:12), health will be good (Isa. 33:24; Jer. 30:17), and the righteous will know no oppression (Isa. 14:1–2).

E. The End of the Millennium

Myriads will be born into the world over this long period of 1000 years. Sin and rebellion against God will arise throughout the earth. When Satan is loosed from the abyss he will be able to gather an army, in number "as the sand of the sea." He will go to war against Jerusalem, but fire from heaven will devour his hosts (Rev. 20:7–9).

It is then that the execution of God's long-standing judgment of the devil will be consummated. He will be cast into the lake of fire to "be tormented day and night forever and ever" (Rev. 20:10). See *notes* at Isa. 14:12; Rev. 20:10.

8. *The Final Judgment: The Great White Throne*

Satan has now been judged. The wicked and unregenerate dead, not only those who died during the millennium but also all who have died in their sins since the beginning of human history (cp. Rev. 20:5), will be raised and brought before the great white throne for judgment (Rev. 20:11-15, where see *notes* at vv. 11,12). The Lord Jesus Christ will judge them (Jn. 5:22).

So all the unregenerate dead, no matter how important or unimportant they may have been, will stand before Christ. None of them will be able to plead mercy through the blood of Christ. They will be able to offer Him only their works. It is the way some of them always wanted to be judged—by their so-called good works or good lives. The books of heaven will be opened and the records of the lives of these unfortunate people reviewed. But another book will be opened, the book of life, in which the names of all who have died in faith are written. None of those who stand before the throne will have his name in the book of life. None of their works will be good enough. So every one of them will be cast into the lake of fire, to join Satan and the two beasts there. This is the second death, from which there is no reprieve, no escape, no resurrection. See Rev. 20:14, *note*.

9. *Eternity*

After the final judgments of men and angels, the heavens and the earth will be purged (2 Pet. 3:10, where see *note*). With this purgation the day of the Lord will end, and a new heaven and a new earth will come into existence (Isa. 65:17; 66:22; Rev. 21:1). See Rev. 19:19, *note*.

The question arises: why should the heavens need purging? The answer is that Satan had access to heaven (Job. 1:6; 2:1) until he was cast out by Michael (Rev. 12:7-10).* There must be no trace of defilement left anywhere (cp. Rev. 21:27).

A. A New Heaven and a New Earth

There will be a new heaven, the new Jerusalem descending from the heaven of old (Rev. 21:1-2,10). This will be the dwelling place of God (vv. 3, 22; 22:1, 3, 5). All the true worshipers of God from every age will be there—an innumerable company of angels, the Church, all righteous men who have been made perfect (Heb. 12:22-24; Rev. 21:12,14). See Rev. 21:2, *note*; cp. *note* at Heb. 12:23.

It appears that the new Jerusalem will be on the earth, a new earth which will be the everlasting home of the vast population who live on from the millennial kingdom into the eternal kingdom, all of whom will have been redeemed. Revelation 21:1—22:7 presents a great mystery concerning which there are a number of interpretations. Perhaps no one has the complete answer, for there is much here that the finite mind cannot fully comprehend. But whatever the precise location of the new Jerusalem will be, it will be God's dwelling place. Wherever He is, is heaven.

B. Christ Will Reign

Scripture states that at the end of the millennium the Lord Jesus Christ will deliver the kingdom over to God the Father, and that the Son will be subject to the Father, "that God may be all in all" (1 Cor. 15:24-28, where see *note* at v. 24). But the Bible also says that Christ's kingdom is an everlasting kingdom (Dan. 7:14, 27; Lk. 1:33; Rev. 11:15; cp. 2 Sam. 7:13; 23:5). Furthermore, it is predicted that the saints will "reign forever and ever" (Rev. 22:5). They will not reign apart from reigning with Christ. It must be inferred, therefore, that the kingdom which the Son delivers to the Father is but a part of the universal kingdom of

*See Ch. V, p. 46.

God (which it is), and that it becomes absorbed by the everlasting kingdom, over which the Son will be appointed to His rightful place as King.

C. Nothing But Blessedness

Finally, in the new heaven and the new earth there will be nothing but blessedness. God will dwell with His people. He will wipe away all the tears of the ages past, and all things will be new. There will be no more death, or sorrow, or pain, or poverty. No sin will be there, no curse. The throne of God and the Lamb will be there. His saints will serve Him, beholding His face forever and ever.

INDEX

Index

NOTES

NOTES

NOTES

NOTES

NOTES

NOTES

NOTES

NOTES

NOTES

NOTES

NOTES

NOTES

NOTES